It's Just Money,
So Why Does It Cause So Many Problems?

By
Karen J. Lee
CFP®, CLU, ChFC, MSFS, AEP

Advance Praise for
It's Just Money, So Why Does It Cause So Many Problems?

While everyone may have financial issues and problems, many people do not know how to solve them. Karen Lee's book *It's Just Money, So Why Does It Cause So Many Problems?* helps you deal with the most difficult financial issues in life, from drowning in credit card debt to divorce, and she gives useful advice and practical resources to help you recover and survive.

Jordan E. Goodman, America's Money Answers Man,
author of *Master your Debt* and *MoneyAnswers.com*

Karen Lee stands among the vanguard of financial planners who understand that a healthy financial condition is rooted fundamentally in a healthy relationship with money. Her insightful book leads the reader successfully through the frequently difficult terrain where money and personal psychology intersect. The expertise she offers provides guidance on the journey toward true financial wellbeing.

Joe Lowrance, Psy.D., Clinical Psychologist and
President of *FinancialPsychologyCeus.com*

Karen Lee's knowledge of finance is exceptional, but it is her keen insight into human behavior that makes both her and this book an excellent resource that will help people take a hard look at their money lives and change for the better. She is a fabulous presenter and her on-air personality comes through as non-judgmental and simply wanting to help people succeed financially. The book is a must-read for anyone trying to find a balance between money and happiness.

Nadia Bilchik, Editorial Producer, *CNN: Your Money*
and President, Greater Impact Communication

This delightful book teaches financial truths through storytelling. Reading it feels like having a conversation with a warm and financially wise friend. The author, Karen J. Lee, shares stories that offer an honest, instructive guide to that uniquely human place where our emotions meet our money.

Robin Applegarth, Publisher, *TheSilverPurse.com-Helping Women Build Financial Security*

Having been in the financial services industry for over 25 years, I can tell you that it is the advisor who truly understands both the logical side of investing as well as the human elements who helps people most. Karen Lee is one of those advisors who truly gets it and, through this engaging book, she shares her insight into the emotional dimension of money while teaching the practical application of basic financial planning principles. *It's Just Money* is a must read for financial advisors and the general population.

Janine Wertheim, President, Securities America Advisors, Inc.

As a communications professional who has worked for over twenty years helping independent financial advisors find their voice through published works such as books, white papers, newspaper columns, magazine articles, broadcast interviews and public appearances, I was sure I'd "heard it all before" when Karen Lee approached me and said she was writing a book about money problems and how to fix them. But now, having worked with her for over two years to write and produce this book and secure other media interviews, I can tell you that Karen Lee brings a real gift with this book, *It's Just Money*, to those who will take the time to read and digest the wisdom it contains. I am proud to be a part of Karen's creative and production team.

Marie Swift, President, Impact Communications and author of the forthcoming book *Become a Media Magnet: Strategies* **and** *Advice for Do-It-Yourself PR*

It's Just Money isn't just a financial book; it's a life book with a personal touch. Karen Lee has a way of sharing authentic, heart-felt stories that will really make a positive impact on how you look at money and financial planning.

Rob "Waldo" Waldman, author of the *New York Times* **and** *Wall Street Journal* **bestseller** *Never Fly Solo*

Karen Lee's book, *It's Just Money, So Why Does It Cause So Many Problems?*, is the antidote to the shame and disappointment people often feel about their own money story. In engaging style and format, she confidently catalogs and unpacks the spectrum of money woes with kindness and deep understanding. No matter one's personal experience, her sound advice inspires a practical and hopeful way forward.

**Lynn Montei, Lynn Montei Associates,
Coaching and Management Consulting**

Karen's passion to help people with financial counseling comes across loud and clear in her book, *It's Just Money, So Why Does It Cause So Many Problems?* It provides wisdom and insight through stories about people who may sound a lot like you. The stories are very interesting, but most important are the lessons they contain that make it easy to understand and relate the finance principles to one's self. I highly recommend it!

Marsha Friedman, CEO of EMSI Public Relations and author of *Celebritize Yourself*

With great wisdom and compassion, Karen Lee's new book offers fresh insight and clarity around the most common money issues and dilemmas that people grapple with daily. Woven with wonderful numerous, engaging stories, Karen offers new perspective and advice on how to better understand our frequently precarious relationship with money. This book can really make a difference in your life!

Deborah Price, CEO and Founder of The Money Coaching Institute and author of *Money Magic: Unleashing Your True Potential for Prosperity and Fulfillment*

Karen Lee has not only "nailed" the biggest reasons people encounter money problems ... she exposes them and provides the solutions by sharing numerous examples of the various money problems with practical examples. Read these money stories and you will almost certainly find one or more that is totally YOU, your spouse, your kids, a good friend, etc. The book is easy to read. It's not laced with jargon, and the pages fly by as you read story after story of people who sound just like you and/or the people in your life. You will find it hard to put down because you want to read about the next person or couple's money challenges. This book is a MUST read for all-including all professional financial planners!

Donald Patrick, MBA, CFP®, Managing Director, Integrated Financial Group, and author of *Keep Your Nest Egg From Cracking*

Karen Lee's book tells realistic stories about people, money and personal change. Lee is a financial expert who in another life could have been a powerful therapist. She understands that to make positive change in our lives around money, we need to change our financial approach and our emotional and psychological experience. *It's Just Money* gives us succinct, wise insight and targeted advice on just how to make such changes, so we can lead more satisfying lives-financially and otherwise.

Barbara Nusbaum, Ph.D., Clinical Psychologist, Financial Psychologist

In Karen Lee's book about finances, she identifies the real problem-the relationship that we have with money. *It's Just Money* is one of the most original books I have read in a long time. It is fun enough to capture your attention, and concisely presents how we can all manage money better. A good read for anyone who wants or needs to gain better insight into something we all have to do in modern society -manage our financial resources.

Arjun Chanmugam, MD, MBA

Karen Lee compassionately bridges her expertise in the world of financial planning with her insight and understanding of the deeper psychological issues people have with money. Through engaging stories, Karen opens the door to what is often as taboo a subject as sex. Readers will find they are not alone in their struggles with money. Hopefully, they will feel more comfortable seeking professional guidance. If they're lucky, they'll find someone as warm and caring as Karen!

Linda Baird, MA, LPC, Certified Hakomi Therapist

It's Just Money is not only extremely informative but a very entertaining read. Yes, Karen Lee has made that scary five letter word, money, explode off the pages in a down-to-earth, real-life way. I wish I had this book when I was in my twenties, because whether you have money or not, money buys you choices and this book gives you a wonderful, refreshing approach to finances and the choices you have that could make your life a lot less stressful if you are armed with this knowledge. BRAVO!

Aurea McGarry, Author of *I Won't Survive, I'll Thrive*, Motivational Speaker and EMMY Winning TV Show Host of *www. LiveYourLegacyTV.com*

Dedication

This book is dedicated to everyone who has ever struggled with money—whether those money problems come from a lack of money or an abundance of money. Whoever you are, you are not alone. I hope this book helps you find peace with your relationship to money, while you enjoy health, love, and happiness in the ways that matter most to you.

In Memory

Marcus N. Bressler — Beloved Father

T. Girard Lee, Jr. — Beloved Father-in-Law

Acknowledgements

Writing a book has been a long-held dream for me. I knew I had something to say—hopefully, something that could make a difference. I am motivated to touch more people and help them improve their lives. I had numerous insights and stories from having worked as a financial advisor for over twenty years. I started keeping a journal to capture my thoughts.

That journal grew and grew, but it did not resemble a book until I started sharing my dream and working with Leslie Swid, Richard Koreto and Marie Swift at Impact Communications. I am grateful to this talented team—who also helped me get the initial PR wheels turning in my career—for helping me shape and publish this book.

I am also very grateful to Olivia Mellan, who took time out of her busy life to read this book and write the foreword. I've admired her work as a psychotherapist, and author of multiple books on money for some time now. I am proud to have her publically validate mine.

A special word of thanks to all my cheerleaders, without whose support I might have decided to give up: Madge, Don, Eve, Wanda, Scott, Amanda, Janine, Rusty, Steve, Pat, Irene, Kathy, Kim, Deb, Lise, Nadia, Josh, Fredricka, Marla and Mindy, and Margo.

A big shout out to my Money Coaching Girls—Lynn, Linda and Barbara—and much appreciation to Deborah Price for her insights during the Certified Money Coaching curriculum.

Mom and Dad: Thank you for instilling in me some incredible values about life and money. I would not be the successful businesswoman and mother I am today without the good examples and guidance you provided during my formative years.

Daniel and Julia: Thank you for putting up with your over-achiever Mom and for supporting me in pursuing my dreams. You are two bright and shining stars in my life.

Eric and Lisa: Thank you for always being there and supporting me. I love you guys.

Ken: It's been quite a journey as husband and wife. My life changed—and is eternally for the better—the day I met you.

Finally, I gratefully acknowledge all the people who have shared their stories and their heartaches with me over the years. Thank you for allowing me to be a part of your life, if even for a brief period of time.

Foreword
By Olivia Mellan

The collapse of the economy in late 2007, and the resulting burdens of overextended credit, underwater mortgages, and market losses have brought our relationship with money to the forefront of people's minds. While the aftermath has been painful for many people, there's always a silver lining in any negative situation. The barrage of shocking news was startling, even for the most financially responsible. The significance of what seemed like a tidal wave of events was a wake-up call for many.

As someone who has worked as a money coach and psychotherapist for many years, I've watched and chronicled the way people think about and behave with money when certain situations occur. Not everyone responds the same way to the same set of circumstances. Much of what we do with our money hinges on decisions we made or things that happened to us when we were in our formative years. Understanding why we do what we do is very useful.

Back in 1983, my first money psychology partner and I were preparing workshops and exploring useful topics for the general public. He made the following statement and changed the entire direction of my life: "You know, we probably should do a workshop about money, because money is still the last taboo in life. People have an easier time talking about sex and childhood trauma than they do about their money." Those words hit me like a thunderbolt! I realized that any time money came up in my psychotherapy office (either with an individual or with a couple) it was as if there were ghosts sitting all around the room— my ghosts and the clients' ghosts. Absolutely no one was talking about the elephant in the room—MONEY!

From this "aha" experience, we coined the term "money harmony" and decided that we needed to invite people to look at their ongoing lifelong relationship with money in the same way people look at their relationships with people. By getting them to discuss where the imbalances were, what fears, anxieties and strengths they had, we could help people forge a new relationship with their money—one that would be healthier and reflect their goals, values, and integrity.

Money psychology grew until it constituted half of my professional identity. Somewhere in the first few years of money therapy, financial planners started coming to my workshops and saying, "All planners should know about this work." To that end, I have been speaking to financial advisor groups since the late 1980's, and I've been writing for *Investment Advisor* magazine since 1996 in hopes of creating more "therapeutic educators" out of financial planners.

When I met Karen Lee I found a kindred spirit whose passion to help others matched my own. Karen's mission of teaching people about their dysfunction with money grew out of two decades of trying to help people with their money lives, and realizing that there was simply more to money than simple math. Karen's passion to help others coupled with her expertise in math and understanding of human nature provided her with the ingredients of a financial advisor who is a natural "therapeutic educator." Whether working with clients, public speaking or getting her message out on TV, Karen's charisma and enthusiasm helps people of all walks of life look at their money issues and make changes for the better.

With the publication of It's *Just Money, So Why Does It Cause So Many Problems?* there's finally a book about financial planning that reads like good book of short stories! It's user-friendly, filled with stories and life lessons that make it a true pleasure to read whether in small chunks or all at once. Rather than being another "how-to" book about finance, *It's Just Money* provides wonderful insight into why people do what they do with their money.

It is gratifying for me to meet a financial advisor who is trained and understands the powerful coaching role that planners can and should have with their clients. Financial planners have the opportunity to help people meet their deeper life goals and confront their fears and irrationalities armed with information and valuable tools to make changes. This book is filled with real money stories about real people you can relate to. Karen's willingness to share her own money journey with honesty and vulnerability helps readers feel like wayfarers on the road with her to what I like to call "money harmony."

When Karen and I first met, I shared the thunderbolt experience in 1983 that led me to become an expert in money psychology. She told me that it resonated with her experience over the last decade, culminating in 2008 with the beginning of the financial meltdown. She had become acutely aware in her practice that people's relationship with money had a direct impact on their possibilities for financial success. With the collapse of the economy, she immediately recognized that from a consumer point of view, it was the dysfunctional relationship with money that had so many people suffering under the burden of over-extended credit and mortgages they couldn't afford. She felt a powerful need to speak out about these issues so she could help people recognize their underlying money issues and turn their lives around.

Karen's commitment in this lively, engrossing book is to finally eliminate the taboo aspects of money talk so that individuals and couples alike can recognize their money issues and transform their money lives into ones of true abundance, fulfillment and "money harmony."

Enjoy the journey with her!

Olivia Mellan
www.moneyharmony.com
Professional speaker, writer, money coach, business consultant and psychotherapist

Disclaimers

This book presents numerous examples of a variety of situations designed to illustrate how an individual's emotional relationship with money can impact their financial needs. The individuals portrayed in these situations are hypothetical in nature and do not portray the actual experience of any one individual client nor are they a reflection of the results that can be obtained by any current or future advisory client of Karen J. Lee. All investments involve risks including the loss of principal invested.

Contents

Introduction
The Formative Years: Confronting the Mystery of People and their Money Lives

When I was a young girl, I remember having a moment where I thought I heard God speak to me. I didn't hear any voices, but a feeling came over me and I distinctly *heard* a message. I would have other moments like these in my life, but this was the first one I remember.

It was absolutely crystal clear. I was standing in a parking lot of a grocery store, waiting for my mother to finish her shopping. The sun came through the clouds and shone on my face and I got the very clear message that *I was supposed to do something important in my life that would help a lot of people.* I was 14 years old. As the years went by and I had to make decisions on going to college and choosing a major, this thought would lightly tap on my mind. I would ask myself, "Is this direction I am choosing going to allow me to help people?"

When I was trying to pick a college and a field of study, I found myself being sidetracked from that purpose. I grew up in a family that was highly accomplished and educated. Both my mother and father went from high school directly into college and would eventually both go back to school to earn Masters Degrees in their fields. My older brother was in medical school at Vanderbilt University. My sister, following in Dad's footsteps, was halfway through an engineering degree at University of South Carolina. It was expected that I would pick a major in a profession versus entering into a liberal arts program.

1

I was interested in psychology and, although it sounds a bit nerdy, I had been reading *Psychology Today* magazine at the age of twelve. Yet I couldn't see myself as a psychologist.

My dilemma was that no professions appealed to me, or seemed to meet my purpose of wanting to use my work to help others. One morning I was reading a college catalog that detailed all the different schools the university had to offer. I was especially intrigued with their description of the School of Architecture. The description was of a career that blended science with the creative and seemed to provide an opportunity to impact the world and the surroundings in which people lived. I thought: "Perfect!! I'm great in math and science, and I've always enjoyed drama and creative writing."

While in architecture school, a few things became terribly apparent. I was far better in math than most of the other students, and not nearly as gifted in design. But with no other direction in mind and the feeling that I had to finish no matter what, I stuck out the five years at Tulane's School of Architecture (lovingly referred to by students as the School of Archi"torture").

All in all I've never regretted those years. First of all, I met my future husband and we have two fantastic kids. I met and kept some of my dearest lifelong friends. And I got to experience and enjoy the incredibly fun and decadent city of New Orleans, an absolute high point of my life.

Another thing I learned in architecture school that I would count as one of my greatest life lessons was the skill of discipline. It was widespread knowledge that architecture was hands down the toughest degree at the school. I have often thought to myself when times were tough, "If I can make it through architecture school, I can make it through anything."

I had two jobs as an architect, both of which taught me valuable life lessons: the most important one had to do with being female. One of the female architects at my firm had just had her first child. After her maternity leave she returned to work asking if she could work

I had two jobs as an architect, both of which taught me valuable life lessons: the most important one had to do with being female.

part-time. This was in 1986 and she was told unequivocally NO. It was either full-time or nothing, so she made the decision to quit and stay home to raise her child. She became one of my many female friends who would later make the same decision. I knew then that architecture, while a great field of study, might not fit well into my vision of my future.

Even more disturbing was that I certainly didn't feel that I was making a difference in anybody's life. I knew within two years of practicing architecture that it wasn't going to be the career of my lifetime. At that point, I went looking for a new vocation.

From a job I didn't like, I was able to construct a description of a job that would fulfill me. I needed to work directly with people, not behind a desk. I needed to feel like I was helping those people and making a difference in their lives. I needed to be my own boss, and have a lot of freedom and flexibility. I wanted a situation where within five years I would be able to work part-time, because that's when I wanted to start my family. And it would be helpful if there were an emphasis on math skills, because I was exceptional in that area.

I began a career search that led me to conduct informational interviews in areas such as marketing and public relations. Five different people with whom I interviewed suggested I consider sales. Sales? People in my educated family did NOT go into sales.

But where was I to go at this point? So, I considered sales ... architecture related sales like floor coverings, windows, doors and such. Everyone wanted to hire me but there was no way I'd consider it, primarily because I really didn't feel like I would be making a difference in people's lives.

So my search continued. One sunny Sunday morning, I came upon an ad for a financial service representative. "Must be a disciplined self-starter, like helping people and be interested in unlimited financial potential." I sent my resume.

The company requested an interview. I went on a whim, really to figure out why a financial service firm would be interested in someone with an architecture degree. At the interview they explained, "if you can make it through architecture school, you can make it through this."

Financial services, they explained, was not brain surgery; it was about perseverance and, in fact, most people fail. They quoted statistics that over 80% of the people who try it drop out within three years. I wasn't overly concerned with those stats. One thing my parents instilled in me was a level of confidence in my abilities. Those statistics were no more than a challenge for me to try it and succeed. More importantly, it met my criteria: Total flexibility (this is of course why most people fail), straight commission (there were no fee-based planners back then) so my output would equal my input and, most importantly, I would be helping people plan for their financial futures—a noble undertaking!

I launched my financial planning career in October of 1987—two weeks before the stock market crash of '87. It didn't matter to me; I barely knew what a stock market was.

Those early years really were horrific. I worked ridiculous hours including nights and weekends. I worked with people who were not genuine in their desire to take care of themselves financially. I worked with others who were serious, but were using me only as a tool to gather information and had no intention of giving me their business. I felt like quitting at least a hundred times in my first year in the business.

But I had glimpses of moments when I knew I was helping people. I actually got thanked and hugged and told I was making a difference in their lives. I knew at the end of that first year that I had found my niche in life. A few of those special clients from twenty years ago are still in my life today and I treasure them.

The years would pass quickly, and I enjoyed much success. But over time I found myself becoming disenchanted with my work. It didn't make sense to me. I had become, in my eyes, incredibly successful, earning far more than I ever had planned on. After the first five years I had gone part-time, and had started my family as well. By any stretch of the imagination, I had the perfect job. I was earning well over six figures a year by the end of my first decade while working around twenty hours a week. How could I be unhappy with my work? Perhaps I was simply impossible to please, high maintenance, and had unreasonable expectations?

Then it started to hit me. Where was the drive for helping people that I had early on in my career? My original passion had waned. For 15 years, I had been doing financial plans for people who seemingly wanted to get help to plan for their financial future, yet it had become apparent to me that a few things weren't adding up.

For one thing, it often seemed that I cared more about my clients' financial life than they did. On too many occasions, clients didn't do what they said they were going to do, or followed some of my advice but not all of it. In addition, it felt to me that although I had certainly helped people, and I'm sure I'd made some difference in their lives, I couldn't really count many financial success stories.

More and more, I found myself intrigued by some of the bizarre decisions people made over money and purchases. In fact, I found myself downright frustrated. As I grew more mature, I realized that people's relationships with money were varied and in many cases, pretty messed up.

I started asking questions of my new clients about how it was growing up in their family in relationship to money, to try to understand what made them tick. We started having really good conversations. I found myself—and my clients—more engaged and energized, simply by talking about what they did with their money and why.

This insight helped me see that all the "how to" books written about money and investing would never truly be able to impact people, until they were able to uncover the roots of what money meant to them. People carry emotional baggage about money from their childhood and, without a doubt, it impacts their adult lives and how they deal with money.

Somewhere along the line, I decided that the best way for me to help the most people would be to share the experiences I'd had with innumerable people—and the insights that helped me understand why most people would ultimately succeed or fail financially. My daily journal would become the basis of this book.

The stories I will tell in this book will, hopefully, strike a chord with you. Perhaps you will see yourself in some of them and ask questions such as, "Is this how I relate to money?" "Why do I do the things I do with money?" "How can I move past today's difficulties and get on firmer footing?"

Let me ask you a few more questions right now: Do you buy things you really can't afford? Horde money? Resist working with an advisor? Fight with your spouse over money? Fail to save for the future when you know you should? Do you know someone—someone close to you—who does some of these things?

Until you can understand WHY you do what you do with money, know how you feel about money and see what void money or stuff fills in your life, you will have a difficult time moving forward and realizing financial success. So whether you are reading this book to better understand yourself or someone you love (or just the human psyche—something I've always found interesting), these are good questions to ponder.

Throughout this book, I will share with you my own "Money Story" in the hopes that reading about my personal thoughts, challenges and ultimate success will inspire you. And so that you can understand my money psychology, I have written a little bit in the early portion of this book about my parents, my upbringing and my married life with Ken. After that, I'll take you through many tales and descriptions of other people's money lives, pointing out some lessons to be learned and providing other professional insights along the way.

Of course, this book—while it contains dozens of stories about other people and how they behave with their money (both the good and the bad)—is really all about you and your life. I hope you will see a few things about yourself, people and money that will empower you going forward.

Mom and Dad: Poster Children for Financial Planning

If you ever read *The Millionaire Next Door,* the best-selling book by Tom Stanley, then you already know the story of my Mom and Dad. Although Stanley did not specifically interview my parents for his book, he describes to a tee my parents' relationship to money, spending and investment in all of its wonderful—and sometimes infuriating—detail.

Let me tell you their story.

Dad was born in Cuba to parents of eastern European descent. From what I've been told, they lived in near poverty, subsisting on a ten-pound bag of rice as the basis of most meals for the week.

In 1942, they were able to come to America, thanks to a sponsor, and start afresh. My dad's father, my Grandpa Isaac, first worked in a leather coat manufacturing shop, cutting leather. Eventually he fulfilled his American Dream by purchasing a dry cleaning store. He managed to put two children through Cornell University, who then started families of their own. My father graduated with an engineering degree, which would lead to long-term stability in the workforce with a decent income stream. Years later my father earned his Master's in mechanical engineering from Case Western Reserve, while raising his family.

My mother was born in Brooklyn, New York, in 1932, the height of the Great Depression. Her father was a shoe salesman who died in his early 30s when she was only seven years old. This left her mother, my Grandma Rose, to support her only child by herself, as Grandma did not remarry until after my mother was married. Rose worked as a bookkeeper in New York's garment industry. My mother also attended Hunter College and graduated with a degree in education, pretty much the only choice other than nursing for a woman of her generation. While working and raising three children, she earned a Masters Degree in education and taught high school economics for the remainder of her working years.

After my father bought my mother her engagement ring, he was left with only $1.54 to his name! But they were both working and of course scrimping and saving as people who've grown up relatively poor know how to do. They made a decision that they would save and invest my mother's paltry teacher's income. Her intent was to stay home with her children when they were born, as the teacher's salary would never offset the cost of daycare. My mother and father were married in 1954, and had my brother in 1957, so that was three years of saving. Then my Mom stayed home for the next eleven years until her third child, me, went to kindergarten. At that time she started working again and continued to work another 22 years as a teacher. Throughout those years, my parents continued to save and invest her paychecks.

We never lacked for food or clothing, and we always knew we'd go to college one way or another, but we still felt growing up that we didn't have much money. This was mostly due to the way my parents made decisions around money and spending. Their attitudes towards money were always based on fear of not having enough.

Similar to the profile of the millionaire next door in Thomas Stanley's book, our home was adequate, but not the nicest in the neighborhood. It always seemed that my friends had more "stuff" than I had. We bought our clothes at Kmart, and this embarrassed me. Our cars were always used and my parents would drive them for years and years before replacing them. When chickens were on sale at the grocery store, but limited to two per person, my mom would take all us kids and line us up with two chickens each so she could come home with eight chickens at the sale price. I'd stand there with my two chickens and my $2.00 hoping to become invisible. We never had the newest electronic gizmos. When we went on vacation and pulled up in front of the motel, the three kids were told to duck down in the back seat so we wouldn't have to pay an extra occupancy surcharge.

I didn't realize until years later that they did have money—their savings and investments—but they were committed to living on my dad's income. They always conducted themselves as if things were really tight. And since they never had the newest of things, I perceived our family as "poorer" than the neighbors or my friends. Obviously this upbringing would directly impact me and my relationship to money and spending, as it would my siblings.

One day, after I'd become a financial planner, my father dropped the comment that they had a multi-million-dollar net worth. My initial reaction was, "How the heck did that happen?" But of course, I knew.

I look back on my upbringing and realize that my parents taught me to value money by buying things on sale. They taught me to save for the future and, inadvertently, to be scared about not having enough money, which is why I have always lived beneath my means.

My parents also, without realizing it, taught me how to enjoy the money I do have today. Once I found out the

My parents also, without realizing it, taught me how to enjoy the money I do have today. Once I found out the amount of wealth they did have, and calculated how much they actually needed to support their lifestyle, I couldn't understand why they didn't spend a bit more.

amount of wealth they did have, and calculated how much they actually needed to support their lifestyle, I couldn't understand why they didn't spend a bit more. My father nobly wanted to leave it for the children, but clearly there was more to it. The truth is that they are still scared that there will never be enough.

I noticed, however, a dramatic personality shift in my mother when she was in her early 60's, and I asked her what had happened to bring about the change. In the past she had been very uptight, and now she really had a lighter, more carefree nature about her. Had she been through some therapy, or was she taking some medication? No. She said she had come to a point in her life when she knew they had "enough" money. She now struggles with wanting to loosen up and spend more. But my father simply cannot break out of the poverty mentality, and this is an ongoing challenge for both of them.

My folks still have a multi-million-dollar estate. I believe the only debt they have is mortgage of maybe $150,000 on a Colorado vacation home, which is probably valued at $600,000. They bought this house as an investment in 1996, for $330,000 after their primary home was paid off. My mother pushed for this, but it almost put my father over the edge. Although he's 81, my father still is working as an expert in the nuclear power industry.

Their battles continue in the following ways: My father is a very large man and extremely uncomfortable in small spaces. In addition, he and my mother love to travel for business and pleasure. With their net worth and extremely low expenses, they should always fly first class and rent a full-size rental car when they travel, but I think it would kill my father to pay for first-class tickets. Of course, with all their travel, they regularly get one upgrade to first class. My Mom sits up there alone while Dad crams into his seat in coach, unwilling to pay for another upgrade. But they seem to be okay with it.

My mom still clips coupons and my dad will spend three hours looking for the cheapest airfare. Several years ago they bought a new Lexus SUV. When I congratulated my father on buying not only a luxury car but also his first new car, as opposed to used, he was very offended. He said, "That's simply not true—in 1953, while in the army, I bought a 1953 Chevy, and in 1963 I bought a new Pontiac."

What conclusions can I draw from all of this? I think an appreciation of the value of money is one of the greatest gifts my parents could have given me, in addition to the value of hard work and perseverance. I am who I am today, and have the wealth I have today, because of them. But from their struggles I learned to be a little more reasonable. Financial planning helped me to see that I could plan for the future and still enjoy some of the fruits of my labor today as well.

That said, my husband Ken and I still have fights about the use of our wealth, but more on that in the next chapter.

Lessons Learned

1. By living on one salary, a couple with two incomes can set themselves up for a lifetime of prudent saving.

2. For good and bad, children observe their parents' attitudes and habits surrounding money, and it affects their own attitudes and habits.

3. Habits are hard to break, even when they're good habits. After a lifetime of saving, it can be hard to spend even when you have plenty of money.

It's Just Money

So Why Does It Cause So Many Problems?

Because financial behaviors are so closely tied to
our upbringings and our psychological profiles,
it can become very difficult to change them.

Karen and Ken: Our Married Journey

To understand ourselves in relationship to money we have to understand the circumstances of our childhood and how we reacted to them. Since I've told you about my childhood, let me fill you in on my husband Ken's.

Ken's parents were born into upper-middle-class families. His father became an architect, and his grandfather had been a builder, so perhaps the family was predisposed to investing in real estate. Indeed, Ken's father saw it as one of the better investment vehicles. As you can imagine, Ken has *always* wanted to own and invest in it.

Ken's dad eventually owned his own company and mom stayed at home and raised their four kids. Ken was the oldest and only boy. Over the years of our marriage, and my career in financial planning, I have queried Ken as to what he remembers about money in his childhood. Like me, he always felt like there was enough money, but he didn't feel "wealthy." He has only one memory of his mother complaining that there wasn't enough money "to go to the grocery store and feed all these children." Beyond that, he doesn't really remember money being a source of conflict in his family, or even being a subject that was discussed openly. Dad had always handled all the money decisions.

In my early years with his family, I was in awe on my first Christmas with them because the gift giving was beyond anything I had ever experienced before. Having shopped with my mother-in-law, I noticed that I go directly to the back of the store to the clearance racks, while she gravitates to the newest things on display.

I met Ken in college, at Tulane University. We were two of the "poorest kids" at a "rich kids' school". I think we were the only students who didn't have cars. We both chose to work for some extra spending money and we rode our bicycles when we went out.

When we were first married, I let Ken handle the bills. He would get very worked up every month over how much money went out the door to pay the bills. Over time I started handling all the bills and investment decisions as it simply caused Ken too much stress. To me, bills were all on paper and a mathematical game, making sure the checking account balanced; it wasn't "real money" to me. I have often wondered where Ken's stress over bills came from.

It goes without saying that we had very different relationships to money when we first got married, and clearly we'd had very different family situations growing up. Yet one thing we had in common was a fear of being without money.

At my first job as an architect, I earned $17,000 a year. At the end of that first year, I had $1,000 saved. When I moved to Chicago to be with Ken, he wanted to buy some camping equipment and didn't have enough money to pay for it all up front. He charged it on a credit card and paid it off in two to three months. I was appalled! Never in my life had I put something on credit that I could not pay off by the statement date. As a married couple, we would never again have any debt other than our house. No credit card bill ever went unpaid at the end of the month.

Within a year of my moving in with Ken, he would have one of his most exceptional years of earnings. Although only 24, he earned $180,000. He was able to put $40,000 into a retirement plan, $10,000 into a life insurance policy and $50,000 into a general savings account. I was impressed: most other 24-years-olds would not have made such mature decisions about money, but would have been more inclined to blow it on a fancy new car and the latest stereo equipment.

It turned out to be a very wise decision, because after that year, Ken's income went down … and down. Ultimately he decided to get out of the business he was in, which was the primary reason we lived in Chicago. We relocated to the Southeast, where the cost of living was lower and we could afford a nicer home.

I would have to rebuild my financial planning practice in the Atlanta area, and Ken would try his luck at being a stockbroker. Again, we were ready to buy a house and start a family, but we made financial decisions around a worst-case scenario: We bought a house that we could qualify for on only one income, and we both continued to drive our older cars. As it turned out, I got pregnant quickly and Ken got disenchanted with selling stocks. He quit his job, vowing to be reemployed within three months, when the baby was due.

Again, life rarely works out as we plan it. Although I went back to work three months after the baby was born, Ken would go another year and a half without working. He decided to go back to school for a Master's in computer science to improve his ability to find work in a new area that held more promise.

It wasn't the most fun time of our life. To be quite honest, I usually refer to it as "The Dark Ages." Besides being emotionally overwrought with a new baby and a husband in grad school, my income was straight commission. We had to watch every penny.

I remember adopting an attitude while shopping of, "Is this a luxury or a necessity?" For two years, this was how we lived our life. But remember, we had bought a house that we could afford on my income only, and we were still driving our old cars. Do you know how many families I've counseled who have to buy a new minivan for the safety of the baby when they just scaled back to one income?

Again, it wasn't fun, but we didn't accumulate any debt and continued to put ten percent of my pay into my 401(k). In fact, I remember suggesting to Ken at one point that we not contribute to my 401(k) until he was back at work. He looked at me and said, "What would you tell your clients?" Of course, I would tell them to keep contributing through thick and thin!

Over time, Ken finished his degree and started to work as a computer programmer. My income went up and within a couple of years I was earning six figures. My more conservative side thought, "Well this could be a fluke, so don't change your lifestyle, just save more." So for the next few years, in addition to putting ten percent of my income into my 401(k) and ten percent of Ken's income into Ken's 401(k), we started saving an additional $25,000 to $50,000 and investing in mutual funds and other investment vehicles.

We continued to stay in the same home, but were considering some renovations. We agreed to pay in cash for any improvements rather than finance with a home equity loan. Though we had to replace our cars to keep up with our expanding family, we always chose a two- to three-year old vehicle with relatively low mileage, and paid cash for them.

I chose to stop clipping coupons at some point because the time I spent on Sundays doing it, and the extra time I spent in the grocery store to try to use all the coupons, had become a burden. I would simply throw a fit if I got to the store and had forgotten my coupons. Truth be told, I had become somewhat of a compulsive saver, and was actually trying to force myself to stop using coupons as a way to help me loosen up a bit on my compulsion to save money—sort of reverse therapy, if you will.

I also learned not to judge people by what they had, as you never really know what their balance sheet looks like based on what they own. But most important, I learned not to judge myself by my belongings or place value on other people's stuff.

I also learned not to judge people by what they had, as you never really know what their balance sheet looks like based on what they own. But most important, I learned not to judge myself by my belongings or place value on other people's stuff.

This has also been a huge area of teaching opportunities with my children. We live in an affluent area in Georgia, but our schools are highly diverse with country club kids, apartment kids and a wide variety in between. My son would come home from a party at the home of a new friend and say, "Mom, they are rich!" I'd ask how he knew that and he'd say, "You should see their house … it's huge!"

Try explaining to a young teen that many people who own that huge house are living paycheck to paycheck and have nothing else to show for their work. Over the years, these conversations have continued and finally my son asked me how much money we did have. That's when I knew he was starting to understand wealth.

By looking logically at money, I was able to achieve by age 40 the peace of mind that I saw my mother get in her early 60's. I don't worry much about Ken losing his job, or having a lower year of earning myself. In fact, when Ken did go a little more than a year with no income as he re-thought his career path, it really didn't affect us or lead to any loss of sleep. And finally I learned that there is a happy medium for me in balancing saving and still enjoying the fruits of our labor.

When laid out neatly like this, it sounds as if we are in total agreement over spending and saving habits. Don't be fooled! Let me tell you about our money struggles. First of all, you have the classic situation where one spouse bears the responsibility for paying bills and making most of the financial decisions. While it generally works for us, there have been many occasions when I've felt enormous resentment over this chore.

Another huge area of struggle—actually, fighting—has been our differing views over the use of our savings. Remember that I learned from my parents to save and invest in the stock market. Ken, on the other hand, wants real estate. He believes that we should be enjoying the fruits of our labor by owning a weekend home on a lake or in the mountains. We have been fighting about this for at least 10 years.

It's not that I don't see the value in owning more real estate; I just don't want to part with the cash. I also hate the idea of increasing our monthly bills for utilities, property taxes, insurance and maintenance on another property. I feel that the financial burden would fall on my shoulders and I don't want any more of this type of responsibility.

For me, a vacation home is something to consider down the road. As far as Ken is concerned, we simply have too much money in the stock market—and he looked pretty smart in 2008 to 2009 with our investments down 35 percent! He would be happier with something tangible to show for our efforts—like property. I see just one more thing to pay for and take care of. I expect to be arguing this one for quite some time.

As you can see by my story, our upbringings had a lot to do with our future financial stability, even though the differences have caused some struggles over the years.

The next chapters will take a look at the myriad of money problems that I have witnessed in other people, from living beyond their means, to fear of never having enough money.

Lessons Learned

1. Marriage, among other things, is a blend of different attitudes about money.

2. You can't predict the future, but a family that is prudent with money even during periods of affluence will find more choices later and greater peace of mind.

It's Just Money

So Why Does It Cause So Many Problems?

Because for better or worse, our attitudes toward money are imprinted on us in childhood.

Chapter 1
Money Problems: They're Universal

Perhaps I'm stating the obvious when I say people have problems with money. No one is immune. People of all races, genders, and socio-economic situations are vulnerable.

I've met couples with problems with money, single people with issues with money, very high wage earners as well as low-income people, people from all religions. Money problems just abound.

People argue over money, politics grow tense over money; when someone dies, families often fight over money to the point of becoming estranged. Couples get divorced over money, and friendships dissolve.

It does, however, seem that Americans have their own particular collection of money problems. Although I have only lived in the US, I have done a good deal of traveling over my life, and I've picked up on a few interesting tidbits about how people in other countries view Americans. Once on a vacation to a resort that was frequented mostly by Brits from the UK, I was asked the following question:

"So, I'm curious … I heard that American's don't pay off their houses … is that true?"

As we discussed their question in more detail, they shared with me that in England, where they lived, the goal of almost every citizen was to pay off their houses. That was a pinnacle of financial achievement. I told this fellow that, sadly, I thought his rumor was true and, worse than that, Americans had started using their home equity as a sort of ATM machine. And interestingly, I explained, I believe that this is a generational shift, in that Americans in the past were more likely to strive to pay off a house and live in it mortgage free; in contrast, over the last few decades, only a minority of Americans strove for debt-free housing.

In another conversation more recently, I had the pleasure of having a driver who was from Somalia talk with me about money. I was on my way down to CNN to talk about the credit card crisis in America, and after I told him what was on the agenda for the day's interview, he said:

"I think it's something in the water! People come to America and just start spending and spending!"

We had quite a laugh over it, but I thought to myself, this Somali limo driver was likely more financially savvy than the majority of Americans who probably out-earn him by many multiples.

Another very telling piece of information is that all these "money problems" are not new. We can go back hundreds if not thousands of years and find that money has been the source of problems as far back as we can find historical writings. People have been misusing money to gain control and power over others for centuries.

We can go back hundreds if not thousands of years and find that money has been the source of problems as far back as we can find historical writings. People have been misusing money to gain control and power over others for centuries.

Looking at the bible, we find references to money and the potential problems it can cause, as well as sage advice on how to value money in one's life. Let's take a look.

Old Testament

Dishonest money dwindles away. But he who gathers money little by little makes it grow.

> Proverbs 13:11

Whoever loves money never has money enough; whoever loves wealth is never satisfied with his income. This too is meaningless.

> Ecclesiastes 5:10

New Testament

No one can serve two masters. Either he will hate the one and love the other, or he will be devoted to the one and despise the other. You cannot serve both God and Money.

> Matthew 6:24

For the love of money is a root of all kinds of evil. Some people, eager for money, have wandered from the faith and pierced themselves with many griefs.

> 1 Timothy 6:10

So what is it about money that makes it so charged, so volatile, so troublesome? One thing we must look at is that money means a lot of different things to different people.

For example, for some people:

- Money is status

- Money is power … the ability to control others

- Money is a measure of success

- Money is security

- Money is a means of buying friends, love, marriage

- Money is a way to feel significant

Why Is It So Hard To Do What We Know We Need To Do?

I like comparing the way Americans handle their money to the way they handle food and diet decisions. Apparently the average person in America is overweight and the number of obese adults and children is steadily increasing, despite the fact that most people realize that you must take in fewer calories than you expend and do a modest amount of exercise to lose weight. Most people even know the basic calorie contents of a variety of foods, and the nutritional basics such as food groups and the food pyramid. So why do many people tend towards overweight? Is it that they like to eat more than they like to be thin?

Money is very similar. In order to build wealth we must take in more money than we spend and save the rest. It's pretty basic: Here is what a family brings in as income, here is the amount you need to save to reach your goals–the difference is what you can spend on life. You don't need an accounting degree to make this work. You will need to make your housing decisions, travel, food expenses, and etc. work within the budget your income allows. It sounds simple, yet, like weight loss, people can't seem to do it.

In order to build wealth we must take in more money than we spend and save the rest. It's pretty basic ... You don't need an accounting degree to make this work.

Is the lure of "stuff" just too great? Is our self-esteem so low that we define ourselves by what we have that others can see? Or perhaps it is the same issue with weight gain. It's the lies we tell ourselves: I eat so healthy (most of the time) ... these crumbs don't really count...just this one bite won't make a difference ... I skipped breakfast so I can double my lunch. Similarly, with money, we say: But I almost always buy clothes on sale ... I have no idea where the money goes ... I must have this new cell phone, smart phone, updated computer, expensive hair cut in the job I have. The excuses and justifications are endless.

Why do people have so much trouble doing the things they know they need to do? Exercise, eat right, floss your teeth—and spend less than you earn, save some money and avoid debt.

Clearly there is more going on here than basic logic. How we deal with money, the choices we make, and how we relate to money is emotional, and self-defining in myriad ways.

It's Not Just Cash or Numbers on a Statement

Money is a powerful force and a personal challenge for many people. It's no wonder financial independence is so elusive for so many people.

Spending money makes some people feel important, exhilarated, and powerful. I have to admit that there have been times when I've been depressed and buying something for myself lifted my spirits, albeit temporarily. So spending money can actually make you feel better, if only for a brief moment in time.

Throughout this book, we'll be exploring the fascinating (and sometimes painful) world of money—and why it causes so many problems.

My Personal Reflections

Chapter 2
Living Beyond Your Means

Without a doubt, living beyond our means is the biggest problem facing people today. The decades of affluence that we have recently lived through changed our views about money. It's been a long time since the fear-based money mentality of the Great Depression and the decades following it.

The credit card, which first emerged in 1949, was the next step towards financial ruin for many people. An entitlement mindset coupled with the ability to spend money we hadn't actually earned yet produced a recipe for disaster; as a result, many people over the past decade crashed and burned financially. Somehow we got the idea that we could always earn more money and pay for things later. Unfortunately, that didn't turn out to be true.

With the onset of the Great Recession in 2008, the pendulum is now starting to swing back to a healthier mindset and corresponding set of financial behaviors. Credit card debt balances are slowly going down and savings rates are increasing. Savings rates in the US reached an all time low of around 1% in 2004, and are now hovering around 6%— but they have not gotten back to the 8-12% savings rates of several decades ago. People are, for the most part however, showing a greater level of fiscal prudence.

Still, old habits die hard, and many people will continue to struggle to live within their means. How can we get over this big problem? I hope the following thoughts and anecdotes will help.

From Living the Good Life to Double Whammy

It's one of the biggest mistakes I see, and unfortunately I see it over and over again: a person—especially in a commission-based sales position—has a great year, with a peak in earnings. The first thing he (or she) does is upgrade his lifestyle or buy some new expensive toys. Ideally, he or she should assume that the great year was a fluke and continue to live life on the current level, at least for a few years, to see if the higher income is permanent. Maybe next year will be a down year for the industry, with lower commissions and little or no bonus money.

Someone I know was in this situation and suffered what I call the double whammy. She had been in the pharmaceutical industry on the sales side and had been doing very well. About 50 years old, she was rebuilding from an expensive divorce, but she was optimistic. Although she was used to earning six figures, suddenly her earnings topped $200,000, and it seemed as if there was no end in sight. The market was giving her above-average returns. Her company was doing well and she had a lot of company stock in her 401(k) plan. She participated in the company's stock purchase plan and had received stock options.

With a net worth approaching $1 million (on paper), she decided to treat herself and buy the car of her dreams, a brand new convertible Jaguar and a new dining room and bedroom suite for her house. The car cost $75,000 and she financed almost all of it, since the financing deals were so attractive.

But shortly afterward, her company reorganized and her great job disappeared. The timing couldn't have been worse for her, as our country entered into the dot com bubble burst of 2000. At 50 years old, and in a tumbling economy, things started to look really bleak.

Most investors have been hit by falling stocks, but for this person, it was a disaster. All her options were underwater, and all she had left was about $250,000 in her 401(k). But what really hurt her was the car. Investments will slowly come back, and you can find lower paying jobs that at least will allow you to make ends meet, but a loan is a loan and the payment continues regardless of the situation. In addition, she had higher maintenance costs as well as insurance costs to contend with. Because she couldn't afford gas and maintenance, she couldn't even enjoy the car on the long road trips she had planned to take.

... what really hurt her was the car. Investments will slowly come back, and you can find lower paying jobs that at least will allow you to make ends meet, but a loan is a loan and the payment continues regardless of the situation.

She never returned to her earlier level of income. It took her years to sell the car and she didn't even get enough to pay off the outstanding loan. Now she's planning to purchase a retirement home at a cost beyond what her current home might sell for, and she's not even ready to actually retire. The justification—a poor one—is that she can buy it at ten percent below market rates, since she currently works for the builder. Of course we're in a real estate slump that may make it hard to sell her current house but, unfortunately, she doesn't seem worried about that.

Lessons Learned

1. Don't make overly optimistic assumptions: One good year is no guarantee of future good years.

2. There's a difference between "real money," like cash in the bank, and "paper" money, like stock options, which may or may not pay off.

3. Don't tie your fortunes too closely to your employer's by investing heavily in company stock: if the company runs into trouble, you could lose your job and your investments will take a hit, too.

It's Just Money
So Why Does It Cause So Many Problems?

Sometimes we are too optimistic about what will happen in the future: one robin chirping on the lawn doesn't make it spring.

Living Beneath Her Means: The Story of Mary B

One day I was introduced to Mary, 38 years old and a very successful executive recruiter. She'd never been married and had no children. At the time she had a long-term roommate who was also a recruiter, who always teased her that she didn't know how to save a buck.

She wanted me to help her get on the road to meeting her goal of having $100,000 in savings. Of course, that wasn't nearly enough money to plan a future on, but for a woman who literally didn't have $100 in the bank, it was actually a lofty goal. The good news was she earned an exceptional income. At the time I met her she was bringing in over $150,000 a year and was expecting a banner year of over $200,000.

After taking a look at her basic expenses (housing, food and transportation), I showed her that saving shouldn't be a problem, and that she might even be able to reach her goal in less than three years. She was so excited: "I'll show her!" she said to me.

She started by making the maximum contribution to her 401(k) plan and simultaneously worked to build up an emergency fund of $10,000. Once she surpassed that amount, she started directing the monthly savings over and above the 401(k) monthly maximum to various investments. She hit her goal of saving $100,000 in under three years. She was elated and very proud of herself.

As I got to know Mary, I realized that she was a spender. A spender can come in many varieties: Some simply deposit their paychecks, and spend down whatever is in the checkbook on a monthly basis. Since they don't take money out for savings first, there is never any money left in the checkbook at the end of the month to save.

Even worse is the spender who spends with no regard to what is in the checkbook. This is the credit card spender, who usually has an attitude of, "I deserve this, and I'll figure out a way to pay for it." With this type of spender, there is no regard for the actual amount of income one brings in each month.

For either type, the biggest challenge going forward, with the lofty goal of trying to help them become savers, is the inability to say "no" to spending or even certain regular expenditures that are not essential.

Even worse is the spender who spends with no regard to what is in the checkbook. This is the credit card spender, who usually has an attitude of, "I deserve this, and I'll figure out a way to pay for it." With this type of spender, there is no regard for the actual amount of income one brings in each month.

Mary was a spender of the first variety, meaning she didn't overspend—she simply spent whatever she earned. In addition, Mary had a variety of "personal expenditures" that she could certainly afford on her current income, but weren't essential. These included regular visits to the nail salon for manicures and pedicures, gym membership with a personal trainer, and eating out regularly with friends.

She also had a penchant for cosmetic surgery. By age 38, she'd already had a face lift and tummy tuck and was planning to have her eyes done.

Recruiting is a cyclical business tied to economic cycles, and the economic slowdown dubbed "the Great Recession" began just as Mary decided to leave the company she was with and go out on her own. Whenever people make dramatic changes in employment, especially to become self-employed, it is imperative to plan ahead for paltry beginnings. She should have doubled or tripled her emergency fund and eliminated as many nonessential expenses as possible.

Unfortunately, although the economy tanked and jobs dried up, Mary's expenses remained unchanged by choice. Although some of our expenses are fixed and regular, many expenses are discretionary and can be reduced or eliminated during tough times.

Before long, she was regularly liquidating assets and requesting wire transfers of funds. Mary depleted her after-tax account in less than two years, and then began withdrawing from her 401(k). I was very discouraged to see this because early withdrawals from qualified accounts like retirement funds are not only fully taxable, but are assessed a 10% penalty as well, if the account holder is under 59 ½. Significantly, one of these "emergency withdrawals" was for another plastic surgery that she *had* to have.

For me, the worst part was realizing that Mary lacked the ability to alter her spending.

During this period of reduced earnings, I still ran into Mary at the gym working out with her personal trainer. Although she had learned to save, she hadn't learned the lesson of living beneath or even within her means. She had not developed the skills necessary to cut back on spending during times of lowered income.

As the withdrawals continued, I regularly asked Mary what she was going to do. Could she downgrade her home? Could she cut back in other areas? The obvious possibility of looking for another job instead of remaining self employed did not even seem to be an option to her.

She finally ran out of all savings. The economy is still depressed, and the high unemployment levels persist. As a result, there are very few open positions for her to fill with her recruits. And as for her future, I have no idea how she'll pay the back taxes and government penalties on the 401(k) withdrawals that will come due.

Lessons Learned

1. It is essential your spending be in line with your income and savings plan. You have to think carefully about which expenses are essential, and which are discretionary.

2. If you're starting a new business, especially in a volatile sector, you need to be especially careful with savings and expenditures. You need a solid business plan that takes into account start-up costs and slow growth.

3. Taking money from a retirement plan is something to be done only in dire emergencies because of the significant tax penalties.

It's Just Money
So Why Does It Cause So Many Problems?

Because sometimes we behave like children and justify our behaviors. We just can't tell ourselves we can't afford something.

The Discipline of Cutting Back

Since my parents were the kind of people who could "squeeze blood from a turnip," you'd expect that the ability to cut back when necessary would be second nature to me. I regularly enjoy the thrill of getting a bargain, and my own story shows the commitment to saving that I've had my whole life. Yet, today I am experiencing emotional upheaval when it comes to reducing my expenses.

As I write this, Americans and people the world over are experiencing tremendous economic pressures and a huge shift in our way of life. The age of affluence might be over, or at the very least, dramatically slowing down. It all began with people starting to live beyond their means with the advent of credit cards. Then, going from ridiculous to absurd, banks gave loans to people for homes they couldn't afford. Dubious inventions, like interest-only and adjustable rate mortgages, cropped up to help people with no money and no income become property owners. Along the way, this rush to ownership led to a long-term run up in real estate prices.

Encouraged by the rapid rise in home values, consumers refinanced other debt into home equity lines to reduce interest rates on debt and gain a tax break. Banks and investment houses packaged and sold these loans all over the place. When the inevitable crash came, it hit everyone, even me.

I've lived beneath my means, still own the first home I ever purchased, paid for all those renovations in cash and never put a purchase on a credit card that I could not pay off at the end of the billing cycle. Even in the good years I didn't loosen up much, although I quit clipping coupons for the grocery store, stopped running to three different supermarkets to get the best prices on all sale items, spent more on travel and gave more to charity.

So I wasn't hit too hard by the recession. Nevertheless, my earnings are tied to the value of my clients' accounts and I saw a forty percent decline in my income. If your boss came to you today and said, "Things are tight, and I need to drop your income by forty percent," my guess is you'd start looking for a new job.

Fortunately, the advantage of living beneath your means is that you have the ability to stomach some reduction in income … but forty percent? And let's face it: we're still trying to figure out how long it will take the markets to come back to pre-crash levels.

Meanwhile, I considered where I could cut back. And that made me angry—irrationally so, but angry nonetheless, as if I should somehow be spared because I had been so good! I felt entitled to what I had been earning.

But I calmed down and realized that now was the time to take action. Where could I cut back? I immediately realized that I had a long-distance service that we no longer used thanks to free long-distance with cell phones. I also noted that I had an extra phone line at home for a fax machine that wasn't necessary.

We have a saltwater fish tank service for our aquarium that comes every two weeks, and for now I have moved them to once a month, spending more time caring for the fish myself. I cut back on charitable giving, although this pains me as I know at times like these charities need our help more than ever. I'm reviewing all our insurance coverage to see if it might be time to raise deductibles and consolidate. I will be calling the cell phone company to see if there is a cheaper rate plan that can work for us.

I am even starting to clip coupons again. Even though it's negligible, it's free money and not a bad habit to relearn. Likewise, if things get worse, I am willing to give up my pink and white nails ($50 a month) and my fresh flower fetish ($30 a month).

Professionally, I can temporarily stop working with my business consultant, and if necessary freeze salaries and bonuses. There are some other niceties I guess we could reduce like gifts we send to clients and such, but I hope it doesn't come to that … my clients deserve all those special little things and I want them to know how much I appreciate them!

But here's my message: We see money as that thing that can buy us *stuff*, and we think that *stuff* makes us happy and that other people love us and want to be around us because of our *stuff*. And that's simply wrong.

---

*... we think that **stuff** makes us happy and that other people love us and want to be around us because of our **stuff**. And that's simply wrong.*

Money is a means to an end. It buys us necessities like food and shelter, but it will never buy us happiness or love. We need to learn to detach from money and see it as a simple mathematical formula: if this is what I earn, then this is what I can spend. Maybe that will be the silver lining that comes out of this crisis. Perhaps Americans will learn the discipline of cutting back and living within their means.

My Personal Reflections

Chapter 3
Carrying Emotional Baggage from Childhood

We all have baggage from childhood around many different issues, but without a doubt, money is one of those issues. In some cases, that baggage can lead to a decent financial outcome, but in many instances that baggage can stand in the way of our financial success and happiness.

This is one of the harder issues to uncover for people when it comes to trying to solve why they aren't getting ahead financially. It's not as apparent as the blatant overspending, or the sense of entitlement issues that many people have.

To uncover these deeper issues, we really have to stop and remember what it was like growing up in relationship to money:

- What do we remember about how our parents handled money?

- Were there conversations or arguments about money?

- What did we learn from watching the grown-ups in our lives?

- Did we model our parent's behavior, modify it somewhat or turn 180 degrees in a different direction in how we deal with money?

- What conclusions did we come to as adults about the purpose money can and should play in our lives today?

- Are we even aware of this money baggage and, if we are aware of it, what can we do to minimize or eliminate it?

Let's explore the emotional baggage that all of us have in one way or another from our childhood years.

Money No Substitute for Love

One of my dearest friends has a great story to share about how her childhood affected her money life as an adult. Her name is Elizabeth and she grew up in Texas, the only child of a wealthy, self-made oil entrepreneur.

Elizabeth had everything in the world money could buy, except the unconditional love of her parents. They were so caught up in their success and money that they had very little time for their only daughter. Much of her time was spent in the company of their live-in nanny—a substitute parent. Her real parents were too busy running around to social events, partying and living the materialistic life.

Elizabeth, now 47, shared with me that she found herself unable to really get ahead financially and couldn't figure out why. As I looked at her finances, I agreed she needed to work on moving forward and building security for her future.

She did not own a home, still had substantial student loan debts, a bit of credit card debt, and no real savings or re-tirement investments to speak of. She had never married and had no children. Although she never really worried much about money, she was just now starting to think about the future and the real possibility of growing older alone and having to support herself.

Since I knew about the family wealth, I asked her about future potential inheritances. She told me that both parents were now gone and had not left her a dime: Her father, once incredibly wealthy, was also a gambler and by the end of his 80-something years, had lost everything and died penniless.

So we began trying to get Elizabeth on the right track financially. She was a bright woman with several college degrees. She had been a scientist for many years, an artist for fun, and currently was involved in providing spiritual healing counseling at which she was quite successful. She made good money and generally was happy in her career.

As I watched Elizabeth over the next year, I noticed a few odd behaviors around spending, which inevitably made her come up short in her debt-reduction plan. We explored what was going on in her mind when she made these irrational spending decisions, and this is what she said:

"Well, when I see something I like, my logic says, 'you don't need that, and for now you can't afford it until you pay down the debt.' But then I think, that's not fair...I deserve it, I want it, I'm gonna buy it."

After that she feels excited, ever so briefly, that she gave herself something she wanted, but then ashamed with herself that she caved in.

We talked a long time about what the feelings were that drove the decision to spend and she said part of it was deprivation. At first I really couldn't get it: Growing up like she did in a country-club environment, how did the sense of deprivation emerge? Then she told me the truth of how it was.

We talked a long time about what the feelings were that drove the decision to spend and she said part of it was deprivation. At first I really couldn't get it: Growing up like she did in a country-club environment, how did the sense of deprivation emerge? Then she told me the truth of how it was.

Her parents doled out money instead of love and quality time with her. Even after she left home they would give her a generous allowance. Still, what she craved was *them*, but they were emotionally unavailable. In later years when

44

she would ask for financial help, she was told, "We gave you everything you've ever needed; you are on your own now." The truth was that her father's business was suffering, and he was scared for the first time in his adult life that he didn't have enough and might run out of money himself. Hearing the truth would have been better for my friend.

Through more conversation, Elizabeth was also able to realize that she sometimes spent money she didn't have to fill inner emptiness and the feeling of being unworthy. She felt imperfect and not what her narcissistic country club mother wanted in her daughter. She had been chastised by her mother for being overweight and having to wear thick glasses.

Her parents taught her some pretty bad lessons about money and parental love. For them, money was a method of control and a mechanism for making and maintaining friends and status. Elizabeth would need to redefine her own beliefs around money in order to build the security that she now desperately desired.

She had spent her adult life despising materialism and denying the importance money played as a tool for security. She didn't want to be like her parents, so when she made money, she simply spent it, feeding her belief that money wasn't important and, unlike her parents, she didn't need it to be happy.

Now age had caught up with her and she was concerned about the future. Fortunately, Elizabeth's story has a great ending. The more we talked, the more she realized that saving money and building a foundation of financial security was the *complete opposite* of what her parents had done. Her familiar spending tendencies were repetitions of her father's behavior rather than repudiations.

She is close to paying off her debt, is building a nest egg for a down payment on a house, and is regularly investing in a retirement plan for her future. She has overcome her irrational spending habits, realizing that they were remnants of a sad childhood and irresponsible parents.

Lessons Learned

1. Our parents' behaviors about money strongly affect our own.

2. We often need someone else to point out that we are behaving irrationally about money—and why—and those behaviors can be overcome!

3. Children need more than money to grow up emotionally healthy and financially strong.

It's Just Money
So Why Does It Cause So Many Problems?

Because our irrational behaviors have deep roots that aren't always visible.

The Eat-Dessert-First Problem

There have been times when I've met people who seem especially kind and friendly and eager for my help—but who display a red flag in our very first meeting. The red flag I am speaking of is an immediate indicator that they might not be successful with their finances. If I know this up front, it might be best not to work with them, but on the other hand, everyone deserves financial help and maybe I can fix them. The red flag is my challenge to overcome.

Such was the case with Ronald and Debbie. I met them in their early fifties when Ron had left one job for a better position with another company in a similar industry. He came to me to talk about his 401(k). He didn't want to leave it with his prior employer, but felt he needed some guidelines as to how to roll it over and invest it.

As always, I suggested taking a comprehensive look at his financial situation rather than just addressing the 401(k) issue. I recommend this for the following reasons:

- No financial decision should be made in a vacuum without the consideration of the entire financial picture.

- Inevitably there are other aspects of a person's financial situation that I can help them improve.

- It should be a financial advisor's responsibility to check over foundation planning, including insurance and liquid reserves, before recommending long-term investments that may lack liquidity or carry other risks.

Ron agreed with my approach—sort of. "That's just fine, Karen," he told me." We'd be happy to let you do that. But let me tell you one thing up front. My Daddy worked his whole life, saving every penny he could in hopes of being okay in retirement. He died six months before his retirement date and never got to enjoy his money. I will not follow in the same path. I'm happy to save some money, but I'm going to enjoy it too while I'm still working and alive!"

There was my red flag! Ron's life experience had led him to believe "you can't take it with you so might as well enjoy it now." Or, as the famous kitchen plaque says: Eat Dessert First. Is that really responsible? No. It doesn't hurt to do that occasionally, but if you do that every day, soon your weight and your health may be in jeopardy.

The years went by, and Ron continued to work and put money in his 401(k) up to amount that the company would match, but no more. He also bought the new cars he loved, and showered the kids and grandkids with gifts. Finally came the day when Ron told me he'd had enough of work and wanted to know if he was able to retire.

I ran the numbers, and based on the budget Ron and his wife presented to me, the numbers looked good. They needed around $7,000 a month net to live on to make ends meet. On a very positive note, Ron had accumulated two pensions totaling around $4,000 a month, and Social Security added another $1,800, so the monthly deficit was only around $1,200 a month.

Ron had accumulated $600,000 in investments, so $1,200 was a sustainable withdrawal rate. In fact, I showed him he could actually draw a higher amount. Ron decided to do just that, drawing out investments at a rate of $2,000 a month. I reminded him of the comment he'd made at our first meeting and told him that my greatest concern was that he and Debbie couldn't stick to the budget they had set out for themselves.

Ron and Debbie assured me that that was not going to be the case. In fact, as neither of their two cars got good gas mileage, Ron decided to replace one with a used Honda for $10,000 to keep costs down. I sent them on their way and held my breath.

When I spoke with them following retirement, they both had sheepish looks on their faces. They brought out an accounting of all their expenditures, which Debbie had meticulously kept, and announced to me that they really needed to increase their monthly investment draw to $3,000 a month. I couldn't understand why, and slowly started to review their numbers, and that's when I saw it:

1. Car Payments: $1,100 a month

2. Equity Line: $600 a month, with $30,000 outstanding

What's this, I asked? I thought you were buying a used Honda for $10,000? Well, they explained, in retrospect, Debbie's car was really getting older, with more than 100,000 miles, and the last time they had it fixed, the dealer offered them an unbelievable deal on a new model … they just couldn't say no. Ron felt they deserved a new car, too, and since financing had dropped so low, he went ahead and financed it.

What about the equity line? It seems there were some things they'd been meaning to do in the house for years and now that he was retired and had the time they wanted to get them done: new paint, inside and out, and hardwood floors throughout the main level. A new screened-in porch was the final thing they wanted to do to make this home the one they could stay in for the rest of their lives.

Another year passed, bringing a severe market decline. I told Ron and Debbie that they couldn't sustain withdrawals at their current levels. I suggested they cut back to $2,000 a month. Unfortunately, they simply can't afford to.

They really are trying to cut back in other areas, but I truly worry they will run out of money. In fact, Debbie's mother is still alive at 95 and there's a high probability that Debbie will live a long time too.

They are not overly concerned about the situation, and feel like it will all work out over time. I'll just have to do the worrying for them!

Lessons Learned

1. We need to get rid of the fairy tales we tell ourselves, such as we may never live long enough to enjoy our savings, so why even bother?

2. "I deserve it" is never an excuse for spending more than you have.

3. You can always rationalize overspending, but that doesn't mean it's a good idea.

It's Just Money
So Why Does It Cause So Many Problems?

Because for many people, the things they buy are essential to their happiness … or so they think.

Allowing Old Fears to Limit Your Options

I've always said that some of my best clients in the world don't necessarily earn so much, but they have a deep-seated sense of fear that they will never save enough money and therefore are incredibly frugal. I like this characteristic because it makes it easier to do financial planning with these folks, primarily because they follow all my advice, live beneath their means and save a lot.

Recently, a couple I've known for decades has been experiencing employment problems. Because they have all of the characteristics above, I am not in the least bit worried about their financial situation … but they are!

The couple is in their mid fifties. They have close to $1 million in savings, their house and cars are paid for and they have no other debt. They do not have children, so their primary concern is their own retirement. There is not a lot of pension income in the future—maybe $500-$600 a month, but if Social Security holds out, they will pull in around $3,000 a month from that.

In addition, they live very modestly: their basic monthly expenses are $5,000 a month. Just simple math would tell us that we can produce enough additional income from their investments to take care of them. They own modest amounts of permanent life insurance and long-term care insurance which provide even more asset protection should one of them die or need home health or nursing home care.

A couple of years ago, the husband, Thomas, lost his job of more than twenty years. He found another but at only sixty percent of the pay he was used to. None of us was concerned as they lived so well beneath their means; it meant that they simply wouldn't save as much. More recently the wife, Trish, lost her job as well. This threw them into a panic. Again, I wondered why they were so worried since their financial plan clearly showed they were fine financially.

Trish came in recently to talk about a few job situations she might be interested in but that paid significantly less than what she had been earning. She's a few years older than Thomas, and quite frankly had had enough of her past occupation. She wanted to work at something less stressful and ideally part time.

I told her she should *definitely* pursue something that made her happier, and that she deserved it as she and Tom had done such a good job setting themselves up for their future. In fact, if she just wanted to go ahead and retire, as long as Thomas worked another couple of years, they would still be fine. Nevertheless, I saw the look of panic in her eyes.

We discussed a scenario in which she worked only five more years at an income so low that between Tom's job and her job, they would have just enough to pay the bills, with no additional savings. I explained that they would still be fine. She said, "Okay, but what about the occasional vacation or unexpected home repair that isn't in the monthly budget?" To accommodate

I told her she should **definitely** *pursue something that made her happier, and that she deserved it as she and Tom had done such a good job setting themselves up for their future. In fact, if she just wanted to go ahead and retire, as long as Thomas worked another couple of years, they would still be fine. Nevertheless, I saw the look of panic in her eyes.*

some additional expenses and travel we took $40,000 out of their current investments, and their financial plan still looked solid.

Curious about the enormous disparities in people's behavior around money and financial planning, I asked Trish, whom I'd know for many years, to tell me more about her childhood. What she shared was priceless! She grew up on a farm in the rural Midwest. She was one of six children, and her father worked labor jobs in addition to farming his own land. They grew their own food, raised livestock and slaughtered them for meat. None of the kids went to college, as Dad didn't believe in it and of course they couldn't afford it. The only value you had was in your work.

Trish started working right out of high school and had been saving like a fiend for the past forty years. I was aware that she and her husband rarely took vacations, but never really knew why. Now I totally understood. For Trish, the only value she learned growing up was that your value is in your work ethic.

This story has a happy ending for so many reasons. Trish was able to recognize that she had options regarding work and retirement. She chose to go to work for a friend who had a business and was looking for help. She negotiated part-time hours, some work from home and a pay scale with incentives. And she knows if it doesn't work out she doesn't have to stay. In addition—and equally important— is that due to their long-term frugality and her ongoing commitment to work, this family needn't worry about their financial future.

Lessons Learned

1. Prudent financial planning does lead to peace of mind, but more than that, it gives you choices.

2. For better or worse, we need to recognize our attitudes about money come from our upbringing.

It's Just Money
So Why Does It Cause So Many Problems?

Because sometimes we aren't prudent, and that can leave us with only a few unpalatable choices as we age.

The Millionaires Next Door: Realizing "Impossible" Dreams

Sometimes the most rewarding financial planning relationships are those that truly transform people's lives and views of themselves.

I'm remembering a couple who had a small, family-owned painting company they'd owned for years and had two of their young adult children working for them. I met them through their CPA, who had told them it was in their best interests to set up a retirement plan for the small company as a way to reduce their taxes in the near term. In addition, since their employees were their children, a classic profit-sharing plan that would have them contribute to all their employees' retirement plans would work well.

When I met them, I told them it would be easy to install a plan for them. Working with the CPA we set it up for that tax year.

Over the years, they continued funding their retirement plan and running their small business.

At one point I suggested that they come to my office and find out about the full spectrum of financial planning services that we offer. They took me up on that, and agreed that they really should have my firm look at everything for them.

We uncovered some gaps in their insurance coverage, as well as found that in the past couple of years, the company's revenues had grown significantly and they were sitting on several hundred thousand of dollars in cash in the business accounts. I asked them why they hadn't made some investments with some of the excess funds, and they admitted that they'd never really thought about it. Apparently they had simply never been in a situation like this before; they were used to simply making payroll and paying the bills at home.

Over the years, the company continued to do well, so we continued to meet, update their financial plans and fund the retirement plan. Although the focus of the funding of the retirement plans was originally a tax strategy, it had accumulated a substantial sum of money.

They realized that their business was actually an asset with value, and that they might start planning on how to exit the business at some point and sell it to the children. This would give the children a true ownership in the business, as well as help subsidize their own retirement.

Their net worth was now well over $1 million, with their investments and their home, but even more if you counted the potential value of the business. I was explaining this to them and showing them the analysis on the computer. At one point, I paused and looked up at them. That's when I realized they were just staring at me—and at the computer screen which showed their net worth.

"Is something wrong?" I said. They looked at me with shock and the wife seemed close to tears.

"No, nothing's wrong," she said. "We just never really expected to be worth so much, to have so much money. You can't possibly know how grateful we are to you for guiding us all these years and helping us plan for the future."

Well you can imagine who had tears in her eyes now … me!

But, for me, the real takeaway was the understanding that because of their modest upbringing and modest lifestyle, these clients didn't have a grand vision for the future. They came from a world where people worked until they died and never really retired. Not only had they miraculously put away enough money that they could retire at some point, they'd left a legacy of a well-established business for their two children to run.

This is, for me, the essence of financial planning! Sometimes planning helps people achieve the dreams they already have in their minds, and sometimes good planning helps them realize things they'd never dreamed of.

Lessons Learned

1. Prudent financial behavior means you have more choices later.

2. Professional financial help can open your eyes to your financial possibilities.

3. When you have a family business, it's best to do business planning and personal financial planning in tandem.

4. Don't let your childhood realities dictate your future possibilities.

It's Just Money
So Why Does It Cause So Many Problems?

Because too often we only think in the "here and now"—we don't plan for the future.

Our Childhood Experience

On a personal note, I've always been a proponent of therapy. I'm sure that sounds odd, especially to those who dread the idea of consulting with a stranger to solve their problems. We should be able to solve our own problems, right?

Whenever I have friends or clients for that matter struggling with marital problems or difficulties with children, I'm the first to ask, "Have you gone and talked with a therapist?"

From addiction issues to relationship issues, I believe therapy can give us a safe place to be honest with ourselves and a productive way to seek alternative solutions to the issues that get in our way of living a life of happiness.

So much of our "stuff" is in some way related to our childhood. Sometimes it's specific things our parents did or didn't do, intentionally or unintentionally. And in other instances it's our past or current life's circumstances or situations that linger, producing fear or other self limiting behavior.

But I must be honest when I tell you that it took me over 10 years as a Financial Planner to realize how our childhood experiences impact our relationship with money. In fact it took me that long to even realize that we all even had a relationship with money. But I am certain at this point in my life that we do.

One of the challenges of this revelation for me was that people don't necessarily come to a Financial Planner to talk about their childhoods. And I'd go out on a limb and say that most Financial Planners don't see the need to open up that conversation. I have a saying, "Financial Planners or advisors are people too." So most likely they have their own relationship with money and possibly their own money baggage that influences them as well.

For many years I personally struggled to understand how a professional athlete, getting a contract to play for perhaps eight million dollars over four years, or a movie star who earns 10 million dollars for a movie, makes the news for being behind in taxes, or worse for being on the verge of bankruptcy. But over time I have come to understand how this can happen.

Take the professional athlete, who perhaps grew up with a single parent, working a blue collar job or living off Grandma or welfare. What money skills were taught to that child? Who was there to turn to for help on how to deal with their newfound wealth? How does anyone who comes from poverty or even from middle class make the adjustment to such levels of wealth?

Sadly, our school systems don't teach personal finance as a required course either. Hopefully over time, this will change, but for now we all need to recognize that we come into our working years possibly ill equipped to deal with money, and definitely impacted by our childhood.

Chapter 4
Dealing with Debt

So you've overspent and you've created debt. Or in some cases you simply fell on hard times and the only way to survive was via the credit card.

While some debt can be good if managed responsibly and well, most debt quickly becomes a yoke around our necks, dragging us down—both mentally and financially.

The good news is you can survive it! You can pay down the debt and there are resources available to help you do that.

But even more important is that you must change your behavior going forward. You must reevaluate your spending and your needs and find a new way of living with regards to money. It is only through this process that you can pay off debt, and move forward to a better financial future.

Let's see what we can learn from other people's stories.

Drowning in Debt and Getting Afloat Again

Young, single, great job—but in debt up to her eyeballs—a woman came to me to discuss her financial situation. She knew what her problem was but couldn't solve it.

Since graduating from college six years prior, she had been with the same company, starting at $32,000 a year. Her salary had gradually increased to $43,000. She lived in a one-bedroom apartment and drove a company car, so all car expenses were taken care of, including insurance and gas. There was no reason she shouldn't be able to live on her income and save, but somehow she had racked up $17,000 on credit cards with absolutely no savings.

She realized she overspent on clothing. Whenever she felt down in the dumps or overloaded at work she hit the mall, just to browse. Inevitably she found some bargain on a top-of-the-line item, and the sale price made it irresistible. She admitted she felt instantly better for having treated herself and for having gotten such a good deal.

But the next day, she always felt rotten, thinking about her debt and how that new charge was only going to make matters worse. She couldn't even bring herself to return the item.

"Can you help me, Karen?" she asked. "I am approaching my 30th birthday, and if I don't get myself under control soon, I'll have nothing to show for my hard work."

I suggested she start with the following:

1. Contact the Consumer Credit Council and get help with her debts. They would work with her creditors and set up a consolidated payment plan she could live with. In addition, they would ask her to go forward on a cash basis only, so she doesn't incur any new debt. (I'd insist on that as well.)

2. Buy some supplemental disability insurance, because at this point her income was her greatest asset, and necessary to pay off debt and start saving.

3. Start putting some money from each paycheck into her 401(k) plan, at least enough to get a full corporate match, so she could feel some instant gratification for starting a saving plan.

4. Put at least $50 per paycheck into short-term savings for emergencies.

5. Brainstorm other strategies she could use to help her relieve stress that don't cost anything: This could be going for a walk, going home to take a candle-lit bubble bath, taking a yoga class at the gym where she already had a membership, or writing out her concerns in a journal.

Amazingly, she followed all my suggestions (although I never asked her what was working for point number 5). Her immediate relief at having a plan and knowing that in 18-24 months she'd be debt-free and on track for savings was evident.

In fact, two years later, she was not only debt free, but she had $2,000 in the bank in liquid savings for emergencies, and over $7,000 in retirement savings in her 401(k). She was ecstatic and glowing.

I was reminded of how empowering financial security can be and the sense of peace that it can bring. She had gotten the message: no matter how fun spending money can be, it was ultimately detrimental to her emotional and financial wellbeing.

Six months later this young woman called me with some incredible news. She had been offered a position with a new company in New York City, a place she'd always wanted to see, and she'd accepted the job. I couldn't have been happier for her. She was increasing her income to over $60,000 with this position and really felt like the world was her oyster.

I was reminded of how empowering financial security can be and the sense of peace that it can bring. She had gotten the message: no matter how fun spending money can be, it was ultimately detrimental to her emotional and financial wellbeing.

I cautioned her about the high cost of living in New York. She said she was fully aware of that and had already set up a budget based on her new income and the cost of some apartments she'd looked at.

We agreed to touch base in a few months once she had settled in New York. It took several months for her to make contact with me, and when six months had gone by and I suggested we touch base, she said she was just too busy with her new job. At the one-year point I tried again to reach out but heard nothing back.

Two years later, I was in New York on a business trip and gave her a ring to see if she wanted to meet for lunch or dinner. She did, and when we got together I saw the look of distress on her face again. She admitted that the difference in the cost of living was much more challenging than she had expected, and sadly she had also slipped back into her old spending ways and run up new debt.

I felt bad for her, but mostly I was perplexed that the memory of the despair of debt had faded for her, as had the peace of mind from being in control of her finances.

I often wondered if she had ever truly worked on finding new ways of coping with stress that didn't involve spending money. Perhaps if she had, she could have avoided a repeat performance of past mistakes.

It's said that the universe will continue to produce the same life lessons until you actually get them right. I hope she is able to get it right the next time!

Lessons Learned

1. Spending can be an addiction, but it doesn't have to be a hopeless situation—there are ways to stop overspending.

2. However, even when you get it in check, overspending, like other addictions, can come back, so you have to be on the lookout for relapses.

It's Just Money
So Why Does It Cause So Many Problems?

Because for many people spending money makes us feel better. Unless we find cost-effective ways to tap into and shore up our emotional lives, we can become stuck in this damaging rut.

It All Looks *so* Good on the Outside

We're told all our lives not to covet our neighbors' stuff, but you have to admit it's hard sometimes. Everyone knows *that family* that just seems to have it all.

I knew one such family. The husband was a well-respected plastic surgeon, doing mostly reconstructive work for breast cancer survivors, and the mother was a gorgeous woman who chose to stay home and raise the children. The doctor was not only a well-known professional, he was also very physically fit. Their neighbors were jealous of their looks and their income.

They lived in a prestigious neighborhood where the women generally did not work outside the home, and if they did, they had daily help at home and nannies for the children. The husband drove an S-class Mercedes, and his wife sported around in a convertible Jaguar. Of course, they kept a third car, an Expedition, for family vacations.

The family was also socially active—throwing a fancy Halloween party every year for adults and children—and the mom headed the PTA at her children's private school. Even the three children seemed perfect. The eldest, a son, was captain of the football team, on track to be valedictorian, and had just been accepted at an Ivy League college. The first daughter had won several equestrian competitions on the horse her parents had bought her, and the youngest child, known as the sweetest child in town, was also doing exceptionally well at school.

I was pleased when the husband called me for a consultation; this appeared to be the start of a smooth and profitable relationship. I also hoped that after he became my client he'd introduce me to other high-net-worth families in their neighborhood.

The first surprise was when the husband showed up alone. Although sometimes primary financial decision makers do come in by themselves, I prefer both in a couple to come see me, at least initially. I started the appointment with the usual description of my firm and the services I provide and quickly transitioned to find out what had brought him to see me in the first place. Next came the second surprise

"I've gotten myself into a little bit of trouble and I was wondering if you might be able to help me get out of it," he said.

I said, "Tell me what kind of trouble we are talking about, and then let's see what we can do to remedy the matter."

He explained that while he was mostly known for working with breast cancer mastectomy reconstruction, he had also done a fair amount of augmentations and reductions. In addition, he was a part owner in a side practice that did liposuction and face lifts. He didn't actually perform any of the latter procedures, but he had provided seed money for a friend's practice and sometimes injected cash for expansion and to offset slow months.

He told me that ten years ago he was earning almost $2 million a year from his own practice and the profit of the other practice. So what was the problem?

When the economy slowed during the dot-com crisis of 2000 to 2002, the side practice took a beating, and he had been forced to use a lot of his own investments to carry that practice. But he said things had gotten back on track during the subsequent four years and although he'd never quite built his income back to those levels, he was still pulling in around a million a year. Again I'm thinking, Okay, so what's the problem?

When the market started declining in 2008, so did his income. A huge amount of his ancillary plastic surgery had evaporated, and the side business was again in trouble. That partnership was requiring more cash infusions from him. After two years of this, he still didn't see things improving.

He had never shared any of his financial concerns with his family. Both his wife and his children were totally clueless that Dad had any financial concerns. And why should they? Nothing had changed for them. His wife still redecorated the house every six years or so, the daughter still had her horse, the son had gotten a new Mustang car (although he really wanted a BMW) and knew the family would be paying the full cost of college.

He had never shared any of his financial concerns with his family ... His wife still redecorated the house every six years or so, the daughter still had her horse, the son had gotten a new Mustang car (although he really wanted a BMW) and knew the family would be paying the full cost of college.

I asked how he had been able to maintain the lifestyle they had become accustomed to without the income to support it. He explained that his house, which was worth $2.2 million, had a primary mortgage of around $1 million outstanding, but when the real estate market peaked, he got an equity line of $500,000, which was now maxed out. In addition, he owed $500,000 on the line of credit for his primary practice. He had maxed out multiple credit cards totaling over $150,000 in outstanding debt, and basically he was simply crumbling financially and emotionally.

While it's hard to feel sorry for someone who earns $1 million a year, I have to be honest: I felt sorry for the guy. I knew I could solve his problem, but it wasn't going to be pretty. There was the possibility of declaring bank-ruptcy, but in lieu of that he could sell the house, and dramatically reduce his family's lifestyle. They'd have hard choices to make, including sending the son to a state school in order not to burden him with $200,000 in student loan debt. He would have to see if he could walk away from being an investor in his friend's practice, thus losing his initial $250,000 investment. Sadly, he had also liquidated every dime in his retirement accounts over the years. Here he stood at 52 years old with not a dime to his name, other than the value of his business and some equity in his home—which in the current market might be nothing.

He told me that the hardest thing for him was to admit he'd made mistakes, and to have to tell his family. I told him I'd heard worse, and somehow that makes people feel better. At least he hadn't lost it all due to a gambling or drug addiction, or a secret family he had been sup-porting. I told him that I was sure his family loved him, and would eventually understand, and that surely he was more to them than simply a paycheck. He and his fam-ily had their health and, in the end, wasn't that what was really important?

Last I heard, the kids had transferred to public schools, the house was let go in a short sale, and the friend's plastic sur-gery practice had shut down. The family was now living in a modest neighborhood. The saddest part was that I heard recently that the wife had filed for divorce.

I wonder if it was the fact that he had withheld informa-tion and basically lied that made her take those steps, or he was simply a meal ticket for her. Regardless, this is just another story of living beyond your means and not mak-ing concessions when income changes, as it is likely to do during bad economic times.

Lessons Learned

1. No one is so wealthy they can't get in over their heads.

2. Cut back when you begin to have financial problems. Don't live on credit, waiting and hoping for things to get better.

3. Financial problems can put pressure on a marriage, but discussing them as they occur is better than trying to hide problems until they inevitably surface when the situation has become disastrous.

4. Don't envy wealthy neighbors; they may not be as rich as they seem.

It's Just Money
So Why Does It Cause So Many Problems?

Because too often our self-worth is tied into an image propped up by cash.

How Do You Teach Others To Enjoy "The Thrill of a Bargain"?

I learned as a young child the value of buying things on sale. Whether it was food, clothing, furniture or electronics, eventually the cost came down, and it was worth waiting for that to happen. But inherent in that strategy is having to wait a bit longer for something you want.

We live in a "I want what I want, when I want it" society, so waiting doesn't come naturally or easily to most Americans. As I've observed the spending habits of friends, family and clients over the years, I've wondered if it would be possible to teach adults what I learned as a child. Could these people learn to wait before they buy?

I believe it is possible to change deeply ingrained behavior: People overcome addictions, criminals become honest citizens, overweight individuals learn to exercise and eat less. There's got to be hope for the over-spenders out there!

I believe it is possible to change deeply ingrained behavior: People overcome addictions, criminals become honest citizens, overweight individuals learn to exercise and eat less. There's got to be hope for the over-spenders out there!

The one thing I'd like to convey is that I certainly don't feel any deprivation while I "wait" for the prices to come down on items. In fact, I really don't wait at all; I just choose to shop only for things that are on sale.

When I grocery shop, I naturally plan our week of meals, based on what's on sale at the grocery store. If I know we need some new furniture, I'll plan to shop at the next major holiday sale, as there's always another right around the corner (President's day, Memorial Day, Labor Day and so on).

Here's an example of how I shop for clothing. It doesn't involve waiting at all; it's just how I shop.

I decided, after a long day of work, to treat myself with a little clearance shopping at a well known department store. Every year I tend to go on a business trip at the end of February, and I decided I needed a few new outfits for the daytime as well as evening events. Conveniently, Presidents Day sales were happening just before this trip, so I was expecting good bargains—which you can always find, especially if you know where to look.

Ninety minutes later I returned, absolutely jazzed at the awesome clothes I got and the deals. My mom taught me my bargain-hunting skills, and let me tell you, it is a skill. I've had many girlfriends beg for me to take them shopping, because they know the kind of bargains they will get if they follow my strategy.

The first thing you do is go *straight* to the clearance racks, usually toward the back of the department. Then you scan all the signs at the top of the racks to see the biggest discounts. Remember: you are only allowed to look at those racks. Don't even entertain the idea of looking at the regular racks. You don't need to. You will find plenty to make you happy on the super discounted racks.

This shopping expedition was especially fun: In addition to the store having racks that took fifty percent off the already lowered sale price, in almost every instance that was already a fifty percent reduction. Then when I checked out, they gave me *another* twenty percent off as a preferred customer. After all the discounts, they were practically giving away the clothes. I was virtually lightheaded at the excitement of getting all these clothes at so little cost.

Basically I took home a fully lined blazer, a silk blazer, a cocktail dress, a pair of dress slacks, two Maidenform bras, a velour Calvin Klein hoody, five cute tops (mostly silk), and jammy pants for my daughter—all for $97. I was so excited that I wasn't going to break $100. Out of curiosity, when I got home, I added up the store's original price for the items I bought and it came to a total of $544.62. I had saved just over 82 percent! In other words, by shopping on sale, I spent only eighteen percent of the clothes' original price at the beginning of the season. Mom would be so proud of me!

I will mention a word of caution about bargain shopping. I've met people who are addicted to buying things on sale. They actually justify their overspending due to the great deals they received on each item. No matter the bargain, spending more money than you have is still over spending. On a personal note, I probably go on one of the shopping sprees described above only three to four times a year. People who might be compulsive spenders most likely do this much more often.

I know I could teach other people the technical way to find a deal on clothes, but here is the more important question: Could I help other people learn to get the rush from getting the deal that I do? I sure hope so because it is a key skill to learning to "live beneath your means," and still have great stuff.

My Personal Reflections

Chapter 5
Windfalls and Excess Income

How could excess income or an unexpected lump sum of money possibly be a problem? These are good problems to have, right?

Not necessarily. Having a lot of income can set us up to create a lifestyle *dependent* on that level of income. And things do change. Salespeople have bad years, companies reorganize and high level positions are eliminated. In the worst case scenario, we could make a career-ending mistake or get injured in a way that leaves us unable to continue to work in our career.

But what about a windfall, like winning the lottery? How can receiving a lump sum of money possibly be called a problem?

A recent article in a Milwaukee Magazine stated that a shockingly large number of lottery winners lose all their money within a few years of winning. National statistics show that about one third of lottery winners file for bankruptcy. Call it poor money management, perhaps, but my take is that there's more going on with windfalls and excess income than just bad math skills.

The following stories will shed some light on these issues.

The Man Who Blew Through $800K

A few years ago, I spoke with John who was referred to me by an attorney friend. John had recently won the lottery. The ticket was worth $3 million dollars! My friend told me that he was extremely concerned about John's ability to handle this incredible windfall and he really wanted him to be sure he talked with a reputable planner as he had no experience handling money.

John had been married to a successful doctor and they had three children, now 18, 20 and 23 years old. Unfortunately, it had been a rocky marriage and even rockier divorce with a long and sad custody battle. In the final divorce, John won primary custody of the children, as his wife had worked long and unreasonable hours throughout their marriage, and John had been the primary childcare provider. Sadly John did not fare as well financially in the divorce and walked away with very few assets, modest child support and virtually no alimony. As happens in some divorces, his highly successful ex-wife was no longer working as a doctor and wasn't forced to help much financially. Indeed, when the children were small, John told me he had spent time on welfare and had had to rely on food stamps. For a college-educated man, this was a tough road. When we spoke, he was employed as a bookkeeper earning only $40,000 a year and it was still hard to make ends meet.

But it appeared that John's ship had come in. A "1 ticket a week" lottery player, John had won a $3 million dollar jackpot. He chose to take the lump sum settlement versus the monthly income for the next 30 years. That amount was almost 1.5 million dollars! For John, who had lived for 15 years just at, or slightly over, the poverty level, this was an astronomical sum. There would be income tax to pay, and some debts to settle, but in the end John would walk away with $850,000 to $900,000 and no debt.

I consider $850,000 a lot of money, and I wanted John to understand how to use it wisely and not go on a spree, spending rashly. I told John and his almost-grown children that although this seemed like a *huge* sum of money, they should be careful and not fritter it away. I felt responsible for guiding them to make prudent decisions, so that the money could take care of them in the future.

I knew that their greatest challenge would be the sense of poverty that John and the kids had grown up with. I believe that is why my attorney friend had sent them to me in the first place. Often when people do without for so long, they can actually develop a sense of entitlement, of deserving better.

As with every conversation about financial planning, we started with goal setting. Their goals were all reasonable and understandable. They wanted to own a home—a first for them—and it would need to be furnished. The two younger kids desired a college education, and John wanted both of them to have their own cars. We also needed to consider John's eventual retirement. In his early fifties, he had health issues, so we set a normal retirement goal of age 65 on the same $40,000 income he was then earning. The present value lump sum he needed to put away today to accomplish that goal was $400,000. I suggested putting that sum of money in a retirement account that would grow on a tax-deferred basis, giving him the highest potential for growth possible and ensuring a comfortable retirement.

That left him with another $450,000 to meet all the other goals. For college, luckily, he lived in a state that had a free tuition program for students who maintained a B average. Room and board would run around $6,000 per year. So we set aside $36,000 to cover two more years for the middle child and four years for the youngest child. For the cars, I recommended the low-end approach: used Hondas or Toyotas at no more than $10,000 each.

I started to see the writing on the wall when the son said he had his heart set on a Hummer and the daughter on a red Lexus convertible. I needed to get them to see that this money was it, until the children graduated college and started working on their own. They shouldn't plan for a second windfall.

Next came the house decisions. My calculations showed John could actually afford a $250,000 home using $50,000 down and carrying a $200,000 mortgage on his current income. I suggested a townhouse or condominium in this price range. However, after all was said and done, he chose a $350,000 single-family home in a new neighborhood. Upgrades included completing the basement just in case any of the children ever needed to come back and live with him.

Once the homes and cars were purchased (and yes, the kids got the cars they wanted), there still remained $300,000 in cash. But of course, the house needed furniture. Most people take it a room at a time and can have empty rooms for years. But John furnished the entire house on one fun trip to the store with his children.

And the spending continued. John really wanted some toys that he had never been able to afford. He also spent lavishly on electronics, computers and a couple of dirt bikes. The children also spent: For example, they each had Dad's gas credit card and were generous with their friends who needed a fill up. And they each had cell phones but could rarely pay their own bills, even though they both worked.

I kept trying to get back with John to make plans to invest the $300,000 that was left, but each time I looked at his account the balance was dropping by the tens of thousands. In one instance, there was over $60,000 gone and John could not account for where it went! He would call me and say, "I just don't know where it's going." We'd stay on the phone and try to write a list of all his recent expenditures and could only come up with $10,000 or $15,000 of the $60,000 that had disappeared over the last couple of months.

This continued. Within 18 months, the entire balance of the non-retirement account was down to under $60,000. (This included the money that was supposed to be for the kids to finish college.) Then, to make matters worse, John totaled his car—and this meant another chance for an upgrade. When he called me from the Mercedes dealership to get my blessing on a $40,000 car, I simply told him I could not justify it. He told me his kids said "he deserved it" for going without for so long.

When he called me from the Mercedes dealership to get my blessing on a $40,000 car, I simply told him I could not justify it. He told me his kids said "he deserved it" for going without for so long.

My worst expectations were coming true. Having lived without wealth for so long, John could simply not hang on to this money. Instead of viewing the money as the key to a comfortable future, it was the payback for a life of deprivation, and was to be spent as a reward for having had such tough circumstances.

Eventually John, tired of my attempts to help him, said I had hurt his feelings with my comments, and stopped calling for advice or even returning my phone calls.

I wasn't sorry to lose contact with him as I couldn't bear to witness the reality that I expected would unfold. I don't know how things turned out for him, but at the rate he was going, he would run out of money within three years, have to foreclose on his house, and once again be reduced to poverty.

In this story we see that it's just as difficult to go from having money to not, as it is to go from not having money to having it. You see it even with people who earn their money: most people who have a great one-year income *immediately* assume it will continue and adjust their lifestyle upwards.

We find ourselves easily intoxicated by wealth and spending. For John and his family, a sense of entitlement following a profound lack of money prevented them from properly managing their financial lives despite my best efforts. As I've said elsewhere, I can only give advice. I can't make people take it.

Lessons Learned

1. No matter how much money you have, it is possible to waste it all.

2. A lump sum of money can be devastating: On some level, we can't grasp this is a one-time deal, and we're strongly tempted to spend as if it will happen again.

3. We're hit with the "deserve" mirage. Whether it's because we've done without for so long or suffered some other hardship, we tell ourselves we "deserve" something, even if we can't afford it.

It's Just Money
So Why Does It Cause So Many Problems?

A perceived or real injustice makes us think we have a license to spend money to make up for the injustice, even if we can't afford it.

Where Does
All The Money Go?

The process of creating financial plans is like solving a puzzle. The "pieces" are the current resources we all have, such as income, investments, any corporate benefits, insurance coverage, potential inheritances and debt. Short-, medium- and long-term goals are also part of the puzzle. The goal is to find out where the money is coming from and—much trickier—where it's all going.

It would seem that the more money a client makes, the easier the puzzle is. It's true that when I meet with someone with a very high income, I get excited about the options. It would seem that the more income a person has, the more savings they could put toward their goals and dreams. However, I continually discover that it really doesn't matter how much a person or a couple *earns*. It's how much they are able to save that really matters. For example, I knew a man who boasted of a seven-figure income. But he was on his fourth marriage with alimony and child support tied to each of the first three. I used to wonder what this man's actual take-home pay was. He probably wasn't able to save much if he had to support four families.

We know where his money went, but for others, we have to look harder. When we take on a new client or even do annual reviews with clients, we always want them to produce an updated monthly estimate of expenses, otherwise known as a budget. But the word "budget" implies a pre-established amount you *must* live within. For our purposes, I refer to this number as the monthly *estimate* of expenses.

Inevitably, when we get people to estimate this number, there is either a shortage or overage projected. That's fine—most people don't know exactly how much gets spent monthly, and a ballpark estimate is all we're looking for. For those who estimate a surplus, the real question is how much of that surplus income are they comfortable saving, and for those who project a deficit, my question is, are they adding to debt monthly? If the answer is no, then we're probably okay. They're simply overestimating their monthly expenses.

The tougher cases are where I find huge disparities between what a person earns and what they claim they spend, with no ability to account for where the money goes.

In one example, I had an initial meeting with a young couple who had an incredible income for people of their age: They had a base salary of more than $200,000 a year—and as much as double that in bonus potential. In my normal optimistic fashion, I created glowing pictures of the future they might create for themselves and their children by saving the bulk of that bonus annually. I knew a young family could live very well on $200,000 a year. By stashing $100,000 to $150,000 a year of the after-tax bonus money, and letting compounding do its magic, in ten years they could be in such a good place they'd never have to worry about money again.

I suggested they use some of the next bonus to create an account that we would add to monthly. However, they didn't follow up and never became my clients. I did see them again around two years later, and when I asked them how they were doing, I was shocked to hear that that all they had saved was the maximum amount allowed in their 401(k) plans (around $16,000 each per year of contribution), which was nowhere near what I had initially suggested.

When I asked where all the income from bonuses had gone, the wife thought it was her fault because she was what I call a "boredom shopper," going to the store daily for one or two items and walking out later having spent $100.

But as I pointed out, even if she did that every day for a year, that would only account for $36,500. Where did the other $100,000 go? Again, they weren't really sure. They started trying to account for the vacations they took and other expenses, but the reality was that they had no idea where all the money went.

They are not alone. I know of another family whose combined family income ran between $800,000 and $1 million annually. Again, in the process of considering if they would use me as an advisor, we collected their financial data. Incredibly, they could only come up with around $300,000 of expenses that they knew of, between two mortgages, the cars, and college expenses for their two children.

Even scarier, over the years they had also accumulated a fair amount of credit card debt. As a result, instead of having two mortgages that were going down each year, the overall debt on each property was going up due to the continually rising balances on their home equity lines. In this case I was adamant that the couple figure out where the money was going, because it would be a waste of my time and theirs to go forward without that knowledge.

As I've said before and it bears repeating, it is not necessarily how much you earn that determines your chances of financial success, but how much you are able to save!

Sadly, I never heard from that family again either. I think that as much as they might have wanted a game plan to help them accomplish their financial goals, they weren't willing to be honest with me, or themselves for that matter, about their spending issues.

As I've said before and it bears repeating, it is not necessarily how much you earn that determines your chances of financial success, but how much you are able to save!

Lessons Learned

1. The first step of any plan is figuring out how much money is coming in and how much is going out. Without that knowledge, any plan is useless.

2. Financial security is not about how much you earn. It's about how much you save.

3. Some people lack the ability to be honest about their spending.

It's Just Money
So Why Does It Cause So Many Problems?

Because we like to spend money—so much so, that we don't keep track of it, or we might realize we're spending too much and have to stop.

Money and Happiness

As a financial advisor, I am always perplexed at the complexities surrounding the old saying that money cannot buy happiness. Of course, many of us have encountered seriously rich people who don't have a true friend in the world, are paranoid about losing their money, have bad relationships with their families, or who are so busy making money they never have time to enjoy it. Whatever their circumstances, all the money in the world does not assure any of us of happiness.

And of course, the ultimate goal in life is to be happy, and thus my personal confusion. I counsel people on the importance of saving money and accumulating wealth for the future. Not having these savings can cause myriad other problems. But we are not assured any particular level of joy due to the wealth that we accumulate. All money can do is help us avoid certain problems.

... we are not assured any particular level of joy due to the wealth that we accumulate. All money can do is help us avoid certain problems.

Today, many people with substantial portfolios have seen them plummet. And even those without portfolios fear the loss of jobs. Whatever group you're in, it might help to remember a time in your life when you had no money saved but were very happy. For me, I recall getting out of college and having my first job. I was just so pleased to finally not have to study! I was truly happy and felt independent and grown-up.

Other times of immense happiness were centered on the purchase of our first home and the birth of our two children. At those times we had some savings but not a lot by a long shot. Our happiness was tied to the events taking place in our lives and our relationships that were growing. After all, that is what constitutes real happiness for most people.

But today, I add up my "wealth" and see that my investments are significantly down in value due to the Great Recession and global market melt-down, and I am depressed. I am frustrated, I am sick to my stomach. And I feel like none of this was my fault. Does this sound like you, too?

The economy and stock market took a hit thanks to the irresponsibility of organizations that loaned money to people who were unable (or unwilling) to see they couldn't afford the loan. And innocents like me (and maybe you, too), who have lived in the same house for 18 years, who always had a traditional fixed-rate mortgage, who refinanced only to lower an interest rate and not to use the home as a cash machine, are suffering the trickle-down effects of those who were less prudent.

But, money does not buy happiness, and I should truly be as happy as I was when I had those extra hundreds and thousands of dollars on my Net Worth Statement. My family is intact. My husband and two kids are healthy and beautiful. We have a roof over our head and, for now, gainful employment. We have a wonderful extended family and so many people we're honored to call friends.

The reality is we are still happy. The challenge is not letting the present state of the economy and our country detract from our personal happiness and joy. And it's hard, because somewhere along the way as both a financial planner and a committed saver and investor, I started thinking that the size of my portfolio determined part of my joy. It's kind of like the number on the scale determining my mood for the day (right ladies?).

I keep telling my clients and myself to focus on gratitude for what we do have and what we can control. Unfortunately, with the negativity that is flying through the media lately, that is a daily struggle!

Chapter 6
Hoarding and Fear of Never Having Enough Money

Of all the money problems I've seen in my life, this is the least harmful from a financial planning point of view. People who are fearful of not having enough money are extremely conservative when it comes to spending and investing. They tend to live *far* beneath their means and save more than a financial plan projects they need to.

Hoarding of *anything* implies some level of dysfunction concerning the object being hoarded.

And fear itself is never a good thing when we discuss money. It can rob a person of the joy of living, as any fear can. It can prevent a person from leaving a job in which they are miserable. It can cause problems in marriage when a fearful spouse dominates the other's ability to enjoy life.

Let's look at some examples, and you'll see what I mean.

Hoarding Money is Another Problematic Behavior

Overspending is a dysfunctional behavior, and so is hoarding. True, it doesn't cause the type of financial wreckage that overspending does, but I still consider it bizarre.

I was once approached by an acquaintance in his early fifties who wanted me to help him with his investments. He had recently been laid off from a job that he had held for more than 25 years. He knew he needed to roll over his 401(k).

He had never been married, had no children and lived in a very modest townhouse valued at $75,000, which was almost paid off. His family had a long history of working for the same utility company that had recently laid him off. Over the years, his father had made some significant gifts of that company's stock to all three of his children.

I took a look at his financial information so that I could make some suggestions about investments. I was impressed: This man had amassed a net worth of over $1.5 million. Roughly half of this came from his father's gifts, and half was money he had saved in his retirement account.

Although that was a good amount, it made me nervous to see that nearly $1 million of his savings was in this one company stock. Yes, it was a very good company, with a 75-year history, no significant downturns and one heck of a dividend. But it has been said that the number one

... the number one mistake in financial planning is too much money in a single company stock.

mistake in financial planning is too much money in a single company stock.

I shared this perspective with him, but he didn't like what he heard. I suggested that he sell *all* the company stock in the 401(k) and roll it over to a fully diversified asset-allocated portfolio. He simply couldn't do it. This corporate stock had supported his father through his entire life and now was basically setting up all three of his father's children comfortably for their lives as well. He could not accept the fact that all it would take was a new CEO or management team to mismanage the company and all his wealth could disappear.

But there was another aspect to this man's story that fascinated me. He had found a new job, working in the garden department of a local home improvement center, earning one-third of what he'd made at the utility company. I showed him how he could use his current investments to produce the additional income he'd been accustomed to at his prior job. He had been earning around $70,000 a year at his old job and this garden center job brought in around $25,000 a year, which is very little money to live on.

Again, he simply didn't see the need. He told me that he could live just fine on the $25,000 a year and didn't need to touch his investments, even as investment income.

So I asked him, "What do you intend to do with all this money you've accumulated? You don't have children to leave it to, you haven't mentioned any charitable organization that you'd like to leave an endowment to, and if you keep working until age 65, and living on your reduced pay, you could possibly have over a $3 million net worth." (Assuming the utility company stays in business!)

Again, he had no answer, nor any plan. Here was a man who simply saved money for the sake of saving money, with no long-term goals for it. Of course, I am an advocate of saving money for the future, and I meet far more people who simply cannot make themselves save enough than those who save for the sake of saving. However, the inability to let go and enjoy the fruits of your labor is also problematical.

It's unlikely that this individual will ever have money problems, but I still see a dysfunctional relationship with money. Just as some people hoard junk because they can't bear to throw anything away, there are also people who hoard money. Here was a man who couldn't allow himself to enjoy the fruits of his labors. You could argue that maybe he didn't require much to make him happy. If that was the case, then I could see many opportunities for him to do a lot of good for other people, whether it be creating a scholarship fund for needy youths or a significant donation to an organization that helped the less fortunate.

My experience with him further reinforced my conviction that money is emotionally based for most people, with very little logic coming into play.

A similar situation can cause family problems, where a "hoarder" is married with children: Dad refuses to spend a dime on anything and Mom has a different perspective, yet is not allowed to buy a new dress or anything new for the children. The children get admonished for not remembering the 15-cent coupon for an item at the grocery store. I've seen relationships destroyed over this type of penny-pinching behavior.

Lessons Learned

1. If money is purely emotional with no connection to logic, hoarding is a possible reaction, just like overspending.

2. We often make investment decisions that are irrational—they may be tied to family tradition and have much to do with the way we are raised.

It's Just Money
So Why Does It Cause So Many Problems?

Because unless there is a plan, money and life can lack purpose and often times joy.

Note: Diversification can be thought of as spreading your investment dollars into various asset classes to add balance to your portfolio. Although it doesn't guarantee a profit, it may be able to reduce the volatility of your portfolio. See also the section in this book on diversification.

When Being Frugal Becomes an Obsession

Julie married Jim because they were so very different. Jim had strong character and a clear sense of direction. Julie admired those traits.

Jim was raised in New York, the only child of a tailor and stay-at-home mom. Jim knew all his life he wanted something better than that for himself. He knew his parents could never afford to send him to college, which he desperately dreamed of, so he started working at 11 years old doing a variety of odd jobs. He'd babysit, walk neighbors' dogs and mow lawns, … anything he could do to earn money. And he never spent a dime of it. His friends would tease him and try to get him to buy things for them, but he proudly told them he was saving all his money for college.

And that's exactly what he did. He graduated from college with a degree in accounting, and immediately went to work at a mid-sized accounting firm in his area. He didn't have a dime of student loan debt, as he continued to work at a coffee shop all the way through college.

He rented a small studio apartment and started to put money in the company retirement account. He also started building up a liquid reserve so he could save enough for a down payment on a house within a few years.

In his last year of college, he met Julie. Julie was studying art history. Jim did love that Julie had a much more carefree outlook on life. This helped him be not quite so serious about everything. After college, Julie started waiting tables at a local diner and taking art classes on the side. She dreamed of becoming an artist.

After three years of dating, they decided to get married. Jim proposed, but told Julie that he didn't buy her a diamond ring because that was a waste of money. They would both get simple gold bands at their wedding instead. Julie was fine with this. She wasn't at all materialistic. She was in love with Jim and having a simple gold band—instead of a big diamond ring—didn't change that.

Julie and Jim combined their incomes and Julie was happy to let Jim make all the financial decisions. He earned a lot more than she did. He knew more about finances and was good at saving.

Two years after their wedding, Jim announced that he'd saved enough money for a down payment on a home. With much excitement, the two started house hunting. But they were quickly disenchanted. In New York, they couldn't even afford a studio co-op on the budget Jim had created.

Two months later, Jim sat Julie down and told her he had a plan. He had researched costs of living in other parts of the US and found that the southeast had the lowest cost by far, especially if they went to a small town. So in the past six weeks he'd looked for jobs in small towns all over the southeast and found one that looked like a fit. The only thing left to do was accept the job, and go down and look for a home to buy.

Julie was distraught. She loved New York. Her family and friends were there, but more so, the art life was rich and fulfilling. She spent most of her spare time at museums. How could she possibly pursue her dream of becoming an artist if she didn't live in a culturally rich location like New York?

Jim told her she was just being silly; she could paint anywhere. And they could take trips to bigger cities to see museums on a regular basis. This way she could see what museums outside of New York had to offer. Julie felt like she had no choice, so she acquiesced and they moved to the small town.

Julie tried to keep an open mind and an adventuresome spirit. It actually went well for a while. A small elementary school in town needed an art teacher, and even though Julie wasn't certified to teach, they let her run the class until they could find someone else.

Jim was happy because the cost of living was so low. He'd had enough money to put 20% down on their new home. He still had savings left over. Although Julie suggested they use some of that money to buy furniture, Jim suggested that there was plenty of time for that in the future.

Eight months after moving, Julie's best childhood girlfriend called to say she was getting married and was having a small simple wedding in New York. Julie was ecstatic, not just because her friend was in love, but because she was homesick and had been begging Jim to allow her to go for a visit back to New York. Now, she thought, he would have no choice but to let her go.

The next night, Jim told her that airfare was outrageous; therefore, they would be driving back to New York. It was a 12-hour drive from where they lived and he couldn't take any time off work, as he had not accrued vacation time and couldn't take leave without giving up pay. Because of this, they would have to drive all night Friday, but they could make it in time for the wedding Saturday night. They would have to leave at the crack of dawn Sunday to get back in time for his work Monday morning.

While generally agreeable, Julie had finally reached her limit. She said to Jim, "Forget it! That leaves me no time to go see my parents and other friends. I'm going and I'm staying a week. You can drive if you want, but I will be flying home."

Jim was furious. He said they simply couldn't afford it. Julie asked, "But what about the money we didn't spend on furniture ... and by the way, I'll also need a new dress and shoes for the wedding." Jim refused to waver, saying they would be driving *together* and she could wear one of her old dresses to the wedding.

The next day, Julie went to visit with an attorney and filed for divorce. She could see the writing on the wall. If she stayed with Jim her entire life and financial situation would be controlled by him. Although originally she thought this would be a good idea, she had come to the conclusion that as good as Jim was with money he had his own problems, and she did not want to be a part of those.

Jim was furious. He said they simply couldn't afford it. Julie asked, "But what about the money we didn't spend on furniture ... and by the way, I'll also need a new dress and shoes for the wedding."

Lessons Learned

1. Sometimes people who appear to have it together with money have other hidden issues.

2. You can be a compulsive saver or a compulsive spender, and both are problematic.

3. Dramatically opposing money behaviors can cause problems in the best of relationships.

It's Just Money
So Why Does It Cause So Many Problems?

Because any extreme behavior has inherent problems. Moderation is the key.

Keeping Money in Perspective: A Well-to-do Doctor

A very dear childhood friend of mine became a pretty well-known doctor in his area of expertise. Over the years I've known him, we've had many wonderful and philosophical discussions about money. He was raised so similarly to me that we often joked that our parents must have been related.

Over the years, this man shared some very personal financial information with me, letting me know just how financially successful he had become. At his peak of earnings, he was making over $750,000 a year as a cardiologist. It wasn't always consistently this high, but even in a slower year he regularly grossed around $500,000 a year. Needless to say, this was a great income.

But I've seen others earning at this level who didn't become so financially set, so I wanted to share a few things he did over the years that are indicative of "people with money."

First, let me tell you about his medical school bills. He went to a private university back in the mid 1970s for four years of medical school. His tuition ran around $10,000 a year. His parents had already paid for his undergraduate education and had stated that medical school was on him. But they agreed to loan him the money for school (I guess that means they had the money, but felt like they had covered what they had planned for.)

Four years later he graduated and owed his parents $40,000. Like most doctors, he had to then go on and do four years of residency and an internship, where he wasn't earning much more than he needed to live on. Then came the day when he got his first real job. At this point, he had married and started his family, but was still living in an apartment. The amazing thing is he paid back the loan to his parents in that first year of true work, prior to even buying a house. He simply hated the idea of being in debt to anyone!

Many years later, he finally bought himself his first luxury car. He bought a top-of-the-line Lexus, the LS 400 series. Of course, he bought it about two years old, so he got a great deal. Last I heard he was still driving that car and it was over 12 years old but, as he told me, it still runs great and gives him no problems.

In the late 1990s, he and his wife and two children made a move up to a significantly nicer home, much nicer than the modest first home they bought. At the time, even I thought he might have changed his cautious financial ways, as this house was priced over one million dollars! I later found out that when interest-only loans came into vogue in the mid 2000s, he refinanced to an interest-only loan but continued to pay handsome monthly payments towards that mortgage, ultimately paying off the mortgage and now owning the house outright.

Occasionally this friend and I travel together with our families. He is the first one to point out when airfare sales are going on, and who has the best rate on a rental car. In addition, on a ski vacation once, he was the one looking for coupons to save on lift tickets and such. Just like me, he gets a kick out of bragging on what great deals he gets on clothing, electronics, and all sorts of things.

Yet let me share another side of this man's personality with you. He is one of his churches' largest financial contributors. I share this with you, because I know that some people perceive people who have great incomes but who still look for bargains as cheap. It simply isn't the case. He just places a high value on money, and a low value on stuff, and therefore is still conscientious about how he spends money.

This man sent both of his children to private universities for under-graduate and graduate school, because he values education. He could have insisted that they go to state colleges to save money, but for him a private education for his kids was money well spent.

You can still value money and look for bargains, and not be cheap. People with money often share a lot of similar behaviors.

His wife, by the way, is another gem. Once on a vacation, she and I went clothing shopping, and I've got to tell you, she spent significantly less than I did. Maybe she doesn't like new clothes as much as I do, but what really impressed me is that I know countless other women, married to well to-do doctors, who blow money like it grows on trees.

And finally, this man who values money to the same degree I do, has often been helpful to me during times of financial stress, offering words of wisdom, like … the title of this book … it's just money!

Being frugal or wise when it comes to spending doesn't necessarily make someone a stingy scrooge. You can still value money and look for bargains, and not be cheap. People with money often share a lot of similar behaviors.

Lessons Learned

1. You can still value money and look for bargains, and not be cheap.

2. You can still have some of the finer things in life if you buy wisely and do not incur debt to do so.

3. You can place a high value on money, but still keep the importance of money in perspective.

It's Just Money
So Why Does It Cause So Many Problems?

It doesn't always have to!

People with Money

Recessions are tough on me as a financial planner. I worry about my clients—not all of them of course, but many. We're still going through one of the worst recessions of my life. The stock market has plummeted, so I pray my clients have the liquid reserves I've preached about to them. The worst thing would be to have to withdraw any funds that are invested in the market for the long term.

The housing bubble has burst, so I hope my clients are not desperate to sell. (However, it's ideal for the potential purchase of a first home, a larger and better second home, or a vacation home for those who can afford it.) In this particular recession and real estate decline, I also worry about my clients who depend on equity lines for cash flow and liquidity as we watch banks and financial institutions tighten up on lending.

And then we have the unemployment numbers, the scariest of all: Which of my clients will lose their jobs? For ninety percent of my clients, the loss of a job for more than a few months will have serious repercussions. Sadly, most don't have the liquid reserves or the discipline to live beneath the two incomes in cases of dual working couples. Few have the ability to cut back significantly on expenditures.

Currently, I have a handful of clients who are out of work. Many are worried—as they should be—but I know one couple who is not: This is a couple in their fifties, with no children, and a house owned free and clear. However, the wife has lost her job and the market remains tough in her field. Still, they're not in a panic because they live dramatically beneath their means and have at least a year of liquid savings.

You may think, "They're probably very rich, and that's why they're not concerned." Actually, they're comfortable but hardly wealthy. Their combined family income is only around $120,000 a year, but they can live on $50,000 to $60,000 if they need to. Some of my other clients and friends might call this couple boring. They don't take fancy vacations, eat out a lot, or buy expensive clothes or jewelry. And they save, save, save ...

All I can say is that this is one time that boring is good! Can you imagine losing half of the family income and *not being worried?* What a blessing!

Over the years, I've found commonalities among the people who have accumulated a decent amount of money.

The first is that many people who have plenty of money are always finding ways to save money, like buying a used car instead of a new one or shopping for clothes or food on sale. They seem to actually place a higher value on money than those who have less, actually being more cautious about spending. This, of course, leads them to— you guessed it—having more money.

In fact, many people with money appear to have less money. They drive older vehicles, live in modest homes, and generally do things on a smaller scale. In essence, they do not spend as much as they could; put another way, they live beneath their means. To this day I am awed by the fact that billionaire Warren Buffet still lives in the same house in Omaha that he has lived in for more than forty years.

Well-off people also tend not to be impulsive when choosing to spend. They extensively research the products or services they're interested in and check for the best prices before making the actual purchases. When it comes to technology, for example, they are more than happy to wait until the price comes down a bit. They're not compelled to be the first to own a new gadget.

... the **behavioral** *aspect of how people interact with and value money is the key factor in whether or not they will become financially stable.*

It's important to note that there is a difference between people who built their own wealth—such as my parents and the other "people with money" that I have referred to throughout this book—and those who were born into wealth. In discussing these prudent financial behaviors, I've been describing people who built their own wealth.

For me, the big question is: "How can we teach other Americans to embody these traits?" As a financial planner with more than two decades of experience watching people interact with their money, it is clear to me that the *behavioral* aspect of how people interact with and value money is the key factor in whether or not they will become financially stable.

Chapter 7
Marriage

In my twenty-three years in financial planning, I've been asked countless times by married couples, "What is the best way to handle the family finances?" I've come to the conclusion that there are both traditional and nontraditional ways to handle it, and depending on the couple, either can work.

Let's discuss the traditional first. When I refer to "traditional set ups," I'm referring to the way my parents and my husband Ken and I have handled finances. It looks like this: One or both of the individuals work. Once married, the couple sets up a joint checking account. Both deposit all earned income into this account. Usually one person pays the monthly bills. Occasionally each may have a separate checking or savings account, but not usually. They have a joint investment account and buy their home together. There is never "my money" or "your money", always "our money". This can still be the case when one of the individuals stops working, usually to stay home and run the house and raise children.

"Nontraditional" will refer to any set up other than the above. The most typical nontraditional is when each person, regardless of individual income, pays half the bills. I've also seen at least one couple who annually calculate what percentage of the total family income each earns and pay that percentage of the bills. (That couple subsequently divorced.) And I've seen many couples who split bills much more haphazardly. For example, one pays mortgage, the other pays all utilities. One pays for all child activities, the other pays all household bills. These arrangements are numerous, and make it difficult for a financial planner to really understand where the money goes.

Regardless of the setup, there's usually some arguing and finger-pointing on how money is spent and who's doing the spending. It gets complicated when one person earns considerably more than the other, or one doesn't have a paying job.

It gets complicated when one person earns con-siderably more than the other, or one doesn't have a paying job.

Often the higher earner or solo income earner wants to control the cash flow, yet the other person usually is in charge of the household, and thus does most of the spending.

The following stories will describe how some couples have dealt with their issues.

The Perfect Couple, At Least Financially!

In successful marriages, sometimes opposites do attract! Take my husband, Ken, and me. I'm dark skinned and sort of ethnic looking. He's the blue-eyed, freckle-faced all-American boy. He's from a long line of great Americans, a descendent of Richard Henry Lee, who signed the Declaration of Independence, while I'm a first generation American on my father's side. Ken's family is quiet and proper. My family is loud and in-your-face. I can tell you that I was definitely attracted to his differences. In fact, I recall saying 27 years ago that he was the most soft-spoken, polite young man I'd ever met.

When opposites attract and marry, however, they usually bring very different money backgrounds and behaviors to the marriage. In the best scenarios, they find the ability to meet in the middle or choose to defer money decisions to the one individual that just seems better at handling financial decisions. Either way, when a good compromise is reached, couples that are opposites can certainly become financially successful.

Every now and then, however, I meet a couple that has the same attitudes and behavior about money. If those are inappropriate attitudes and imprudent behaviors, financial disaster is usually imminent. On the other hand, when the couple comes to the table with good money values, you have a financial marriage made in heaven!

when the couple comes to the table with good money values, you have a financial marriage made in heaven!

Take David and Rachel, a couple with the same religious background, raised in families that were similar in both the way they made their livings and the way they lived their lives. Both David and Rachel worked, one earning around $80,000 a year and the other around $125,000 annually. They were in their forties and childless.

They're both very frugal, maximizing savings in their 401(k) plans. They live beneath their means and pay cash for everything, including their cars and the renovations on their house. The only real difference between the two of them is that Rachel seems to worry more about the future when it comes to money.

She worries that even with their current net worth of more than $2 million, they still might not have enough. She worries about tax rates in the future, health care and catastrophic health crises that could devastate them. David has a calmer nature about it all, figuring that the best they can do is save as much as they can, and then not worry about the future and trust that it will all work out.

I certainly agree with David on this. Financial planning does help you plan for worst-case scenarios, but there really is only so much in life you can control and some things just can't be anticipated or planned for.

Because this couple has such great financial skills, I think it's worth highlighting a few of them:

- They don't finance anything but their house, and save up cash first for all other purchases.

- They continue to live in the house they bought ten years ago, even though they can now afford a more expensive house.

- They buy the car they desire, but usually one that is two to three years old.

- They continue to drive their cars until they are at least 10 years old or have significant mechanical problems.

- They discuss all financial purchases before making the final decision, including purchases that don't affect the other.

- They put the maximum allowable into their retirement plans, no matter what.

- They choose to buy inexpensive things (like wine at $10 a bottle, clothing at thrift stores or at least at deep clearance, even though they can certainly afford to spend more).

- They invest in the markets and stick with a long-term strategy without deviating.

- They choose to ignore future potential inheritances in their financial planning, even though they are highly likely to receive money when their parents pass away.

- They seek outside professional investment guidance, especially now that their portfolio has grown substantially.

- They actually worry that they don't track all their spending and really should know where every dollar goes.

So occasionally it happens that "like marries like" and a financial match is made in heaven!

Lessons Learned

1. Similar attitudes about money—when they are prudent attitudes—can make for a good marriage.

2. Although you can't anticipate every problem, financial planning will help you weather many crises.

It's Just Money
So Why Does It Cause So Many Problems?

Because it is rare for people to marry that have such similar relationships with money.

So You Think You Know Your Spouse

Although money is typically one of those taboo subjects that people don't talk about openly with their friends, if you tell a stranger that you're a financial planner, before you know it they're sharing their financial life with you. I'm sure doctors and lawyers have the same problem. The following story was especially intriguing to me.

I was on a plane, after delivering a presentation to a group of financial advisors titled, "Sometimes I Feel Like a Therapist, Instead of a Financial Planner." The man next to me asked, "So is this trip business or pleasure?" I told him I had just given a talk to a small group of financial planners about the bizarre behavior I regularly see involving people and spending.

He said he knew *exactly* what I meant and started to tell me his story. The man was an engineer-type—practical and methodical about life and about money. He said he prided himself on living comfortably on his pay while his wife had stayed home to raise their three children, who were all grown now and out of college. He'd been a "do it yourselfer" on investing, which is common among engineers, and he appeared to have done a decent job of saving.

With the children gone, he and his wife chose to downsize the house. After finding the perfect new house, he began to arrange for a mortgage,

After finding the perfect new house, he began to arrange for a mortgage, and got a surprise on his credit report. Several problems popped up, which stunned him, because he always paid his bills on time and usually paid credit cards in full.

and got a surprise on his credit report. Several problems popped up, which stunned him, because he always paid his bills on time and usually paid credit cards in full.

The cause of the problem? Multiple credit cards in his wife's name that he knew nothing about. They all had outstanding balances of around $10,000 each, and each month only the minimum payments had been applied. Some had even been late. He was blown away! He had always had near-perfect credit scores in the high 700s to low 800s. How could he have no idea that his wife had these cards, and what in the world had she been spending money on?

She had to come clean: she'd opened these cards one at a time over the years, and spent a little here and a little there on nothing special really. Over time, the bills added up. She couldn't afford to pay them off on the monthly cash flow, and since she didn't want to admit her spending, she just kept it a secret and paid what she could each month.

Immediately wanting to rectify the situation, the man dipped into savings and paid off all the cards, froze her credit, and then to assuage his wife's spending needs, he gave her $400 cash per week to spend as she chose, with no need to account to him about what she spent it on. (This was simply petty cash, as he took care of paying all the other household bills like mortgage, utilities, car insurance and groceries.)

So I'm thinking to myself: $1,600 a month on discretionary stuff—that's a heck of a lot of clothing, lunches out, and whatever else one might use it for. But hey, if this is how they worked it out, and if he could afford it, then okay

Now at this point in the plane ride, I was assuming that this was the end of the story, and they lived happily ever after … but no, he had more to share.

Basically virtually every week, his wife asked for her allowance a day earlier than the week prior; she just can't seem to make the $400 a week stretch to her regular "pay day." When he asked her where she was spending the cash, she told him that she was helping needy families through their church. Now he felt like a heel since she was clearly trying to use the cash to help others … but he knew she had spending problems, so he insisted on her waiting until the day of the week that they had originally established.

One day after a business trip, upon his arrival home, he walked into the bedroom to unpack and noticed that his dresser was gone and all his clothes were stacked on the floor in piles. He found his wife and asked, "Where is my dresser?" She told him that one of the church families had no furniture and she knew he was always complaining that his dresser was too small. So she gave them his and figured that he was due for a new one. In fact, she had already found the perfect new dresser for him and now just needed his okay to go buy it.

At this point, the guy realized she has a big problem and became concerned that it could affect his own financial future and possible retirement. He told me that he is 55 years old, and although happy in his job, he doesn't want to work forever. Also, with the uncertainty in today's job market, he was very insecure about his wife's "problem."

At this point, I told him that in my professional experience, her "problem" sounded more like an addiction, and he said, "Funny you say that, because she's a recovered alcoholic" and hasn't had a drink in 15 years. I shared with him some knowledge that I had about addiction, that many people switch addictions when they try to overcome one, and perhaps, she had switched addictions to spending.

Sadly, the man told me that he had since been to a lawyer to see about divorce, because although he still loves his wife and had been with her almost 30 years, he didn't want to risk his own financial future. Of course, divorce has its own financial challenges, like parting with half his savings and ultimately having to support his wife as well, as she had never worked. He really didn't know what to do at this point.

The bottom line is his wife needs help and although he might force her to seek treatment, he can't control the outcome.

My main questions to readers:

1. Do you have secrets about money?

2. Do you ever make purchases that your spouse never knows about?

If you can't be honest about where the money goes, you have a slim chance of reaching financial freedom in your life.

Lessons Learned

1. Spending can be as addictive as alcohol and gambling. Promises don't work—addicts need treatment.

2. Spending secrets in a marriage will always come out later, and the longer they remain secret, the more trouble they will cause.

It's Just Money
So Why Does It Cause So Many Problems?

Because addiction trumps the most technically sophisticated and prudent planning.

Opposites Attract

Laura and Larry were the perfect couple. Everyone loved them. They were the life of all the neighborhood parties and did the bulk of the entertaining out of their own home. Although Larry was a bit more introverted and shy compared to Laura, he loved how being around her brought him out of his shell. In the three years they'd been dating, Larry's social life had greatly expanded.

Both Laura and Larry worked and had excellent jobs. Larry was a financial analyst with a top five investment banking firm. He made serious money to the tune of around $175K a year. Laura also had a great career as an event planner. Her job provided much more flexibility, some perks like travel, and she brought home around $95K a year.

Both Larry and Laura were career-oriented and loved to travel. They decided before they got married not to have children. Neither of them was particularly tied to the idea of kids, so they decided that being Aunt and Uncle to their siblings' children would be good enough for them.

Larry, being the financial guy that he was, started doing financial planning early in life. Larry came from a family that lived extremely frugally and were big savers. Although not nearly as thrifty as his family, he always saved 10% to 20% of his pre-tax income into a retirement plan. When he and Laura got married in their mid 30's, he already had a nice nest egg of retirement funds—around $200K.

Larry also had a stock portfolio worth around $75,000 and an emergency fund of around $25,000. He'd bought a personal disability insurance policy and a small life insurance policy by the time he was 30. Larry also had purchased a lovely home when he was 25 years old, which had appreciated well over the years. When he and Linda chose to marry, they agreed that the house was big enough for both of them, so Laura, who at the time was renting, just moved in with Larry.

When it came to money, Laura was the opposite from Larry. Laura grew up with a single mother who barely made enough to make ends meet. She never had new clothes, buying everything she needed from thrift stores. Laura's father was never in her life. Her mother died penniless in her early 50's. Laura's attitude when she started making money was one of making up for the past. She *deserved* the finer things in life—the things that she had done without in her childhood.

Laura was a spender. When she met Larry, she didn't have a dime to her name. She was renting a luxury apartment and leasing a BMW. Larry quickly went to work trying to change Laura financially. Laura was self employed so there wasn't a 401(k) plan available, but Larry showed Laura how she could set up an IRA or even a SEP IRA, allowing her to save some pre-tax dollars.

Reluctantly, Laura took his advice and started to save some money for the first time in her life. Larry felt confident that since Laura took his advice on starting an IRA, she was on board with allowing him to guide her in making better financial decisions.

After Laura and Larry got married, Larry put the house and mortgage in both of their names, so that Laura could share in the growing future appreciation of his house. He changed all his beneficiary designations to Laura, and purchased both life and disability insurance for Laura as well. From that day forward, they shared in making payments to the mortgage company and splitting all the household bills equally. Since Larry earned more money than Laura, he often paid for things like date night and vacations, which Linda couldn't afford on her income.

Fast-forward 10 years to 2008. Laura and Larry are now in their mid 40's and still loving each other's company. Laura's business and income had continued to grow, but event planning was stagnating and most companies were cutting back on events due to the Great Recession. Laura's income had basically been cut in half.

One weekend, Laura sat Larry down to have a big talk about finances. Although she felt horrible about this and knew Larry would be disappointed in her, she needed his help with her finances. As her income had been declining, Laura confessed that she had started putting more and more of her monthly purchases on a credit card and had not been paying it off monthly as she had when they first got married. In fact, her outstanding balance was at the limit on the card—she owed a whopping $25,000—and the credit card company had increased her finance rate to 18%. At this point, she was barely keeping up with the accruing interest.

Laura confessed that she had started putting more and more of her monthly purchases on a credit card and had not been paying it off monthly as she had when they first got married. ... At this point, she was barely keeping up with the accruing interest.

Larry was very disappointed and told Laura that they needed to review their entire financial picture, and figure out how to do things differently going forward.

When they sat down with everything, one more piece of financial news came out. Over the last year, Laura had also depleted her *entire* SEP IRA—over $50,000. She was now on the hook for income taxes and early withdrawal penalties, which he estimated at $20,000. Larry was more than disappointed; he was furious. As much as he loved Laura, he was not willing to let her destroy all the financial security for which he'd worked so hard. If he bailed her out this time, would there be another time? And if he did bail her out, he would greatly deplete his own emergency fund, leaving him at risk.

Larry had such a deep-seated need for financial security, that although he loved Laura dearly and she really was his best friend, he actually contemplated divorce to safeguard himself from potential financial ruin. However, as Larry thought things through rationally, he quickly realized that if he divorced Laura, he'd have to pay her one half the value of the home and probably equalize their retirement accounts. He would be far worse off financially in a divorce.

The truth was he really didn't want a divorce. He also knew that Laura had some major money issues she would need to deal with if their marriage were going to work out.

He came to her after a few days with the following offer. Larry was willing to pay off both her credit card and the taxes due to the IRS if Laura was willing to do the following:

1. Combine finances for the purpose of paying bills and allow Larry to monitor her spending.

2. Go see a therapist with him to discuss their financial situation openly and help them through what would most likely be a difficult transition of sharing all spending decisions.

Laura reluctantly agreed, and the couple is still together trying to work things out. It's not been an easy road, and many fights have occurred over Laura's penchant for clothes, shoes and handbags; but big picture, these two are much better off.

Lessons Learned

1. Couples should always discuss spending and savings attitudes prior to marriage to find a common ground.

2. Many times, it is more prudent in marriage to stay together and try to find ways to work out money problems.

3. People can change their money behavior if the stakes are high enough.

It's Just Money
So Why Does It Cause So Many Problems?

Because we keep secrets about money instead of talking about money issues openly.

My Personal Reflections

Chapter 8
Divorce

Divorce is not only one of the greatest disasters that can strike a family, it's one of the worst things that can hit a financial plan. It's right up there with disability and premature death.

When I was in college, I took a sociology class. One of the sections of the curriculum was on marriage. The professor asked, "What is the number one cause of divorce?" Hands went up all over the room and answers like, difference in religion, addiction, sex troubles were shouted out. The professor paused and claimed that money was the number one cause of divorce.

In doing research for this book, I spent some time looking into the current statistics on divorce and although many of the studies are contradictory, and the actual statistics vary, I did come to the following generalizations:

Not all marriages fail for the same reason, nor is there usually one reason for the breakdown of a particular marriage. Nevertheless, we hear some reasons more often than others.

They are:

- Poor communication

- Financial problems

- A lack of commitment to the marriage

- A dramatic change in priorities

- Infidelity

Other causes include:

- Failed expectations or unmet needs

- Addictions and substance abuse

- Physical, sexual or emotional abuse

- Lack of conflict resolution skills

Another article I read stated the following:

Money causes friction, of course. In a study of married couples from 1980 to 1992, seventy percent reported some kind of money problems. When looking deeper at that database, however, they found that those problems didn't necessarily lead to divorce.

Whether or not it's the number one cause of divorce, money clearly is one of the stressors in a majority of marriages. So many of my married couple clients come in and talk during their appointments with me about the disagreements they have over money: This one spends too much ... this one wants to save too much and horde money ... she is always spending too much on clothes for the kids, hair and nails, Botox ... he is always spending too much on electronics, his motorcycle, eating lunches out ...

The reason I consider divorce such a financial disaster is very basic. ... When couples divorce, they now have two homes to support, and the income simply doesn't go as far.

The reason I consider divorce such a financial disaster is very basic. In a marriage you have two people sharing one home, and that home, with its various utility and upkeep costs, is usually the couple's largest monthly expense. When couples divorce, they now have two homes to support, and the income simply doesn't go as far.

When I was growing up, my parents used to fight all the time, but I never recall them fighting over money. (It was usually a mother-in-law.) Nevertheless, by the time I was a teenager and mildly traumatized by all the constant fighting, I would ask my Mom, "Why don't you two just get a divorce if you are so unhappy?" My mother in her infinite wisdom used to say, "Because together we are rich, and separate we are poor."

I thought this was the silliest cop out response I had ever heard—until, of course, I grew up, went into financial planning and saw what a divorce could do to a financial plan. Here are some stories that will help you understand the dynamics of marriage and separation better.

No Pre-nuptial Planning and Mismatched Priorities

No one gets married planning to have a divorce – at least, no one outside of Hollywood. But it happens, and attitudes about finances are often a contributing factor. The time for a couple to clarify their thoughts on earning, saving and spending is *before* they get married. The differences may be so extreme that the couple may want to reconsider marriage plans. In other instances, they may realize they can resolve differences, but only with compromise and counseling. The key is early planning.

The traditional divorce scenario has typically involved the bread-winning husband and the stay-at-home wife who, as popular lore has it, takes her husband to the cleaners. But today, anyone can get hurt in a divorce.

Here's a tale of woe that hinges on bad pre-nuptial planning involving "Diane," who married "Sergio" when she was 25. It was a storybook marriage seemingly made in heaven. A strikingly beautiful woman, Diane was the daughter of an attorney who had his own successful practice. Diane studied law, joined her dad's practice, was very ambitious and was on a path to significant financial success.

She then met a beautiful, blue-eyed young man from Venezuela, whose father (also a lawyer) was a business associate of Diane's father. The two had several joint projects and as a result the two young people were thrown together. Like Diane, Sergio was working for his father's firm as a clerk.

The two dated long-distance, never really getting to know each other because they didn't live in the same state, let alone the same country. But the romance bloomed over the course of six months and they ultimately married and settled in the United States.

All went well for the first couple of years while Diane worked her way up the ladder, on track to become an equity partner. But Sergio lacked both the drive and intelligence for law school. This meant that he would never progress past the point of being an office staff person. She became pregnant after a year or so of marriage and by the fifth year of her marriage had brought two beautiful children into the world.

I had always sensed some latent stress over the fact that, not only were Sergio's earnings quite low, *but he didn't even seem to care*. In the words of the bumper sticker, he'd "rather be fishing."

After eight or nine years, Diane confessed to me that she was miserable. Interestingly, it didn't have to do so much with money, but with their attitudes about it. Diane simply had not gotten to know Sergio well enough while dating and hadn't realized that he wasn't intelligent or ambitious enough to hold her interest. Of course there was more—there always is—but basically the marriage was destined for failure.

After eight or nine years, Diane confessed to me that she was miserable. Interestingly, it didn't have to do so much with money, but with their attitudes about it.

At this point, Diane was earning $250,000 per year while Sergio was earning about $25,000. I never sensed that Diane wanted to divorce Sergio because he didn't earn enough. She wanted to stay married for her boys and for herself. Unfortunately, after a year of counseling, even the therapist suggested that she file for divorce, because Sergio was never going to change.

Their state had a law that decreed that each party of a divorce deserved to live at the standard to which he/she had become accustomed during the marriage. Diane had always followed my advice, maxing out her retirement savings every year, and putting aside additional funds as well. Needless to say, Sergio wasn't much of a saver. They had bought a house at an opportune time and lived in it for ten years; thus is had appreciated significantly.

The financial terms of the divorce were as follows:

In order for Diane to stay in the house, which would minimize the disruption for the kids, she needed to turn over almost her entire retirement account to Sergio. She also had to pay him more than $4,000 a month in alimony. Since she would retain primary custody of the children, he was required to pay her child support. As the amount of support was calculated based on his ability to pay, it was set at only $125 per child per month.

The divorce virtually bankrupted Diane. Yet she'd done nothing worse than marrying too young, without really knowing her fiancé well enough to make a good decision. Although she had built up a net worth of almost $750,000, the divorce left her with only her home and much less income after her alimony payments.

After several years, Diane went back to court to offer a lump sum payment to Sergio in lieu of future alimony, which he accepted. While that cleaned out the rest of her savings, at least she felt like she could make a clean start financially.

I'm happy to tell you that ten years later and in her mid-forties, Diane has not only been able to rebuild her wealth (remember she was a good saver!), she has finally met someone and is engaged to be married.

This man is smart, emotionally mature and ambitious—
and comes to the marriage with no financial baggage. Although he too was divorced, he never had children and his
ex-wife's income was similar to his, so his divorce was not
nearly as financially devastating.

Lessons Learned

1. It isn't so much money itself that can separate a
   couple as their attitudes about it. A hardworking,
   ambitious social worker earning $50,000 and a
   hardworking, ambitious attorney earning $750,000
   might do just fine, as they have the same attitudes
   about getting ahead. The problem in this case was
   that Diane cared very much about getting ahead in
   her profession and Sergio didn't care about his.

2. Have the conversation early. Did Diane really expect Sergio to suddenly become ambitious? Did he
   say he would? Did she believe him? A series of discussions might have saved a lot of heartache later.

3. To a certain degree, you can be a unilateral success. Diane's fiscal responsibility allowed her to
   pay off her husband with a lump sum and bounce
   back later. So even if one spouse is irresponsible,
   the partner can certainly reap the rewards of good
   financial skills.

It's Just Money
So Why Does It Cause So Many Problems?
One cause: Mismatched priorities.

An Average American Divorce

This is a story about a regular family, living a middle-class life, and the devastation that a divorce can cause. This could happen to anyone and all too often does.

Bill and Kate got married right out of college at 22 and 21 years old respectively. Bill was in the automotive industry, employed as a sales manager, and was regularly moved to new territories to help build up struggling dealerships. His career took them to many different states. They both loved the change of venue that the moves provided.

All Kate ever wanted in life was to be a Mom, so she and Bill got to work quickly on creating a family. In the first eight years of marriage, Kate gave birth to three healthy children and was fulfilling her life's dream. The kids were happy and healthy. Her life was full of joy.

Bill traveled a lot in his current territory, visiting all the dealerships that he supervised. Many of those trips were overnights and Kate didn't mind at all staying home with the children. However, as those who travel for a living know, it can get old. Bill was ready to stay home, spend more time with the children and plant some roots.

So when it came time for his next move, Bill made it clear to his company that he really wanted this to be his final move. The company of course said that they understood, they would try to make that work for him, but they couldn't make any promises.

Bill and Kate moved into a lovely home in a great neighborhood where they really felt like they belonged and could stay long term. The school system was outstanding all the way through high school, which was very important. Although Bill earned around $90K a year, they knew that public schools were their only option.

They bought a house for $325,000 with 10% down payment, so they had a mortgage of $292,500. Since they knew they were planning on staying put in this new home, they wanted to make it everything they ever wanted. The house was quite dated, and they quickly got the renovation bug. Home values were rising, so it was a no-brainer to refinance the house after the first two years, and take out enough of the new home equity to redo the kitchen—and what a beautiful kitchen it was: stainless steel appliances, granite counter tops and custom cabinets.

A few years later, with home values literally exploding, they decided it was time to update the bathrooms. This time they simply took out a home equity loan for $50,000 and completed two beautiful new bathrooms with all the bells and whistles. At this point, their home was appraised for $450,000. Their primary mortgage was now $330,000 and the equity line balance was $50,000.

It seemed like life couldn't have been much better.

Kate had always handled paying the bills and used to tell me how great it was that Bill trusted her to handle the finances. They had around $150K set aside for retirement, and some of Bill's company stock that he'd been awarded as incentive pay. Life was good.

One day over coffee, Kate told me that she had some major concerns for Bill. For one thing, she felt like their reluctance to move had compromised Bill's growth opportunities with his company. She and Bill repeatedly discussed the possibility of moving, but they truly loved their home and the kids were well into middle school and high school and wouldn't be pleased about a move.

Bill shared with Kate his growing dissatisfaction with his work, his lack of challenge and actual boredom with the monotony of the same dealerships in the same territory for so many years now. Bill decided to make an offer to his company to travel to an additional territory outside of the one he currently oversaw, and they readily agreed.

Again, it seemed as if the couple had overcome another challenge, until one day while Bill was on the road, a phone call came in on Kate's cell phone. The Caller ID said it was a call from Bill. When she answered the phone, Kate said hello, but there was no answer. Then she heard the telltale conversation in the background and realized that Bill hadn't called—his phone had auto-dialed her number. Instead of hanging up, she listened for a while and what she heard turned her life upside down.

It turned out that Bill wasn't alone that day. Now that Bill was traveling again, he'd started having an affair. Of course, this isn't an uncommon story: Bill was in his mid 40's and after 20 years of marriage, life had gotten boring and mundane. An affair created the excitement that seemed to be lacking in his life.

Kate would have nothing to do with Bill after that deception. She went to a lawyer and filed for divorce. Bill didn't fight her. He actually wanted out of his family life as well. In the divorce, Kate got the house and her fair share of the retirement account and company stock. Bill was to pay child support and alimony as well, but Kate would need to go back to work.

Although devastated by the breakup of her family, Kate and the kids adapted. She found a job as an administrative assistant making around $38K a year. With the child support and alimony, Kate was doing just fine.

Then came the economic meltdown of 2008–2009, with the deep decline of real estate values. But what really hurt this family was the hit to the automobile industry. The worst possible scenario began to unfold. Bill lost his job when his company went through a series of cutbacks. On the meager unemployment check he received, Bill was unable to keep up alimony and the full level of child support. Kate couldn't make her mortgage payment without it.

Then came the economic meltdown of 2008– 2009, with the deep decline of real estate values. But what really hurt this family was the hit to the automobile industry. The worst possible scenario began to unfold.

With much regret, she went to sell the house, which at the peak of the real estate market was appraised for $450,000. The appraisal she got was only $350,000. The outstanding primary mortgage plus the outstanding home equity line was $400,000 (she'd added a bit more to the equity line following the divorce for legal fees and paying off some credit cards she had run up).

She tried to short sale the house, but the bank would have nothing to do with it. In the end, she had to foreclose. That alone was devastating enough, but then she found out that the foreclosure did not wipe out the equity line and the bank was coming after her for that as well.

She had no choice but to declare bankruptcy. Scarier than that is the fact that in this devastating economy, Bill has still not found work. She and the kids are renting a two bedroom apartment, all three kids have gotten after school jobs to help with household expenses, and Kate lives with a constant fear of not being able to pay rent month to month and literally being homeless.

There's no happy ending on this one. Divorce is *always* emotionally difficult but, coupled with a bit of living beyond your means and a bad economy, it can be financially devastating. In retrospect, refinancing of the home multiple times was, ultimately. It was the straw that broke the camel's back for this family.

Gratefully things have improved somewhat in interim, but the devastation that this divorce caused will take many years to undo.

Lessons Learned

1. Living frugally and racking up savings can make a future bad situation less devastating.

2. No one gets married thinking they might get a divorce, but it could happen. So plan accordingly.

3. Using home equity to fund home renovations isn't as prudent as saving up and paying cash for improvements.

It's Just Money
So Why Does It Cause So Many Problems?

Because we tend to live our lives as if nothing will ever change. We live in the "here and now" instead of planning for possible problems that could occur.

Chapter 9
Raising Children

A question I hear regularly is "How do I teach my children how to handle money?" It's such an important question to answer, as it is evident that *what we learn as children* affects how we manage money when we become adults.

I don't think there is only one right way to teach kids values about money, but I'd say there are a few very important guidelines that make for a good start.

Before we discuss some of those options, let's acknowledge that in trying to teach children frugality, parents are up against some very tough odds. First of all there is intense pressure from some kids peer groups. I've heard of stories of kids being teased that they don't have name brand shoes or clothes, or that they don't live in the "best" neighborhoods. This can get so difficult for some children it borders on bullying.

And many of those children, in turn, put pressure on their parents and accuse them of being mean, cheap, or financially unsuccessful. Often parents feel put in the position of going into debt versus disappointing their children. Some parents even feel that they limit their child's social popularity by not buying them the latest greatest clothing, ipod, or cell phone.

As any parent who has raised a child knows, another important life lesson we must teach our children is that people, especially children, can be cruel. And their lives will be full of people who will put them down for one reason or another as a way to build themselves up.

Nevertheless, one of the most important things to impress upon your children, especially if you are well off or not worried about spending, is that money is still something to think about before spending. That is a message that only we can give our children about the value of money. This is an important message, regardless of how much money we might have access to.

I tried to teach my children to wait to buy items until they go on sale. I found this to be one of the most valuable lessons that my parents taught me, and I wanted to pass it on to them. Basically, whenever we go into a store and my children find an item (usually clothing), I ask them if it's on sale. If it isn't, I suggest that if we come back in a few weeks, it will be and they will be able to buy more items.

I tried to teach my children to wait to buy items until they go on sale. I found this to be one of the most valuable lessons that my parents taught me, and I wanted to pass it on to them.

At one time, my son was going through a label-conscious phase and wanted to make sure he had the specific brand of clothing that all the other kids were wearing. Instead of trying to tell him how wasteful it was to be so brand-loyal, I handled it this way: I told him that I bought my own clothes at a department store that had regular sales. I usually spent $20 for a pair of shorts. I would be happy to take him to the store where he wanted to buy his shorts and would pay $20 towards any pair shorts he chose. The rest of what he spent would come from his monthly allowance. He bought two or three pairs from this store, and promptly announced to me that he no longer cared to shop at that store, as it was overpriced!

One method I've heard used regularly by other parents or experts is to give children an allowance. From that allowance they are allowed to spend one-third, save one-third, and give the other one-third to charity. I've seen variations on this, where the one-third that was saved can be spent at the end of the year. This would teach the importance of saving up for bigger purchases. Another variation is to visit a kid-friendly mutual fund website, and actually teach children to invest the one-third they are saving.

One of the greatest lessons my parents used was when I went to college. The first year they bought a meal plan for me that included breakfast, lunch and dinner, and unlimited amounts of food at each meal. By the second year, I told them that the food was awful, and of course, none of the cool kids ate on the meal plan, so I no longer wanted to eat on the meal plan either. They said, "No problem" and proceeded to write a check to me to deposit into my checking account for the exact cost of the meal plan for the semester. They then said, "Spend it however you'd like, but be careful as there will be no more money sent for food for the whole semester." Guess who learned to budget, at the ripe old age of 19?

A few more guidelines for teaching children about money:

- Talk about money.

- Discuss how much you are spending on an item when they are with you. Is it a "good price"?

- Do not, under any circumstances, buy them everything they want, whenever they want it. This is not real life!

- Admit mistakes you've made with money, in hopes of teaching them to do things differently.

- Explain how a credit card works and the appropriate use of one.

- Help them understand about buying a house and what a mortgage is.

- Teach them the value of work by offering to pay them for chores that are above and beyond the normal expectations.

In this section we'll talk about kids and money. Whether you have kids of your own, or children in your life that you care about and can influence, you can make a difference by helping the younger generations learn to manage their money wisely and make responsible decisions.

Blowing It on Baby!

I met Mary and Josh when they were newlyweds and wanted to talk about their financial future. . Their biggest concern was that they had met and married in their late 30s and Mary's biological clock was ticking away. If they wanted children, they needed to get started.

We talked about all the basics, like building up an emergency fund, buying adequate life insurance, writing a will, and getting retirement savings up to speed and allocated correctly in appropriate investments. Both Mary and Josh worked and their salaries were about equal.

Since they were planning for a child, I asked them a series of questions to draw them out. I asked about work plans after the baby came. They decided that Mary would take about three months off and then they'd see how they felt about it. They knew they had to save up income, since she had no paid maternity leave. Fortunately, they had good health insurance that would cover virtually all medical costs and the grandparents would help furnish the nursery. Thinking longer term, they want to be able to pay for four years at a private college.

Mary became pregnant fairly quickly. With two salaries, this family had plenty of discretionary income to fund all the necessary savings for the emergency fund, maternity leave, their own retirement and the baby's college savings. In addition, they had money enough to buy the additional life and disability insurance that they needed. I couldn't have been happier for them and I know they felt great relief at seeing the possibilities for their future.

We agreed to talk again just before the baby was due. Fast-forward six months. In comes a very pregnant Mary with

Josh in tow. The pregnancy was going well, but they did have a few financial things they wanted to update me on.

I was hoping to hear about all the money they'd put into savings, the insurance policies they'd secured and the great new furniture that the grandparents had purchased for the nursery. Instead the update included the following: new debt!

Mary and Josh now had a $33,000 car loan and had taken $5,000 out on the equity line on their house. The emergency fund, which by now should have grown to $15,000, was standing at $4,000. As they explained each of the debts, I started to get the picture: The grandparents had offered to pay for the new crib and dresser, but instead of going out and actually purchasing it, they simply sent a check for what they felt was a reasonable cost for the crib, mattress and matching dresser. When Mary went shopping, she felt like the amount they sent just didn't buy the quality of furniture that she wanted for the new baby. She reasoned that the crib she ultimately bought would last longer and be better for her new child.

Still, that didn't explain the equity line. Apparently, Mary's best friend had started a designer collection of baby bedding complete with matching drapery, and she simply had to support her friend's new venture.

Now for the car loan: I took a big breath and I said: "Funny, you didn't mention to me six months ago that you would need a new car, and the two cars you had weren't really that old. Did something happen?" Josh said: "No, but Mary convinced me that the two cars we had simply wouldn't work once she was hauling around a baby in a car seat." His car was only a two-door, and her car was a bit older and "simply didn't have all the safety features" that the new top-of-the line minivan had. So they traded up to a brand new, fully loaded, seven-seat luxury vehicle.

"Well, what's done is done," I said, "but I'm very concerned about the three month's maternity leave and that you haven't saved up the amount we agreed upon to offset Mary's income during that time." I was told not to worry; they'd reviewed the budget and they really felt like they could live on Josh's income exclusively during maternity leave.

Thankfully, their belt-tightening worked out. The next time I heard from Mary was four months later. Their new baby boy had been born and all was well. But she simply couldn't bear to leave him at daycare, so she'd decided not to go back to work and to stay home full time with the baby. I asked how it was going living on the one income. She told me that it was "very tight" but they were making it.

I never heard back from this couple and I always wondered how it all worked out for them. I'm all about couples making the decision for one to stay home with baby and run the house. In fact, I think in many ways it can make for a much less stressful home life overall. But I felt that this couple had already shown poor money judgment, taking on additional debt at a time when monthly expenses were going to go up due to diapers and formula and such. I would have advised waiting to make any additional purchases until Mary had made a decision about work.

I never heard back from this couple and I always wondered how it all worked out for them. ... I felt that this couple had already shown poor money judgment, taking on additional debt at a time when monthly expenses were going to go up due to diapers and formula and such.

This would not be the first time in my career that I watched a couple "blow it" when the dizzying excitement for the new baby (and feeling compelled to buy the latest and greatest for the little Prince or Princess) overwhelmed people who were usually rational thinkers, so much so that they ended up making very bad financial decisions.

Lessons Learned

1. You have to make a plan to fit your situation—you can't change your mind later and expect the plan to work as well—or at all.

2. A solid financial future is a much better gift for a baby than special custom furniture.

It's Just Money
So Why Does It Cause So Many Problems?

Because our emotions—in time of great emotional change—can overwhelm our common sense, leading to financial problems.

Still Financing Your Adult Children

I was at a cocktail party recently when I got into a conversation with a couple in their late 50's. They were lamenting that "this generation" has it so much tougher than they did. I was curious as to what way they meant, because I've always thought that every generation has some things tougher and some things easier.

They went on to explain that they had raised two children, a son and a daughter, now 28 and 31 years old, respectively. They had paid for them both to go to four years of college at a state university, and each had graduated with an undergraduate degree with minimal student loans outstanding.

In the case of their daughter, she had had a difficult time finding work after college, and ended up taking a job at a local coffee shop. She simply couldn't earn enough working there to support herself, so she lived at home with her parents to save on rent. The goal was to pay off the student loans and build up enough money for a security deposit on an apartment that she could share with a few roommates. The other hope was that she find a better paying job, again pay off student loans but be able to move out of the family home more quickly and possibly get an apartment by herself.

The situation wasn't ideal. As most people know that when a child has experienced the freedom of living away from home, it is hard to go back and live under mom and dad's roof again. Nevertheless, they made it work for two years until she found a better job and moved out.

The couple went on to tell me that the next year was really great for them. They were empty-nesters for the first time, and they were loving life. They had only one year left of tuition to pay for their son, and they were on track to retire as they had planned to at around 60 years old. They were rediscovering the fun in their relationship, and looked forward to the day that they could stop working, begin traveling, and enjoy more time together.

Then their son graduated from college and had the same situation as his sister. He couldn't find a decent paying job in his field of study and had to take a job waiting tables. Unlike his sister, he couldn't fathom the possibility of moving back home, so he immediately made plans to rent an apartment with three other guys, which he could swing on his restaurant pay.

As I listened to their story, I was wondering what the problem was. It sounded to me like both children had eventually become independent from the parents, so why the lamenting?

Well as usual, there was more to the story …

Their daughter had moved out, but two years later, came home for a visit and told her parents some awful financial news. She had run up a sizable credit card bill of over $10,000 AND had gotten behind on her student loans. The creditors were on her back. When they delved more deeply into her financial situation, they realized that she was spending more than she earned and hadn't saved a dime for emergencies, let alone for her retirement one day. They chose to help get her back on track by paying off both the credit card debt and the student loans, but this had put them a little behind for their own plans.

Their son had actually never moved beyond the restaurant job, and because the couple really didn't want a child living at home with them at this point in their lives, they just made it a habit of "helping out" when he needed them to. Apparently the "helping out" amounted to a couple of hundred dollars most months, and an occasional couple thousand, when he over spent on credit cards, had car repairs, or whatever.

But the real problem was that they had not fulfilled their own dreams of retirement. They hadn't built up quite the savings their financial adviser suggested they needed, and their adviser insisted that they would not be able to go into retirement and keep helping the children financially without the probability of messing up their own financial plans.

... the real problem was that they had not fulfilled their own dreams of retirement. They hadn't built up quite the savings their financial adviser suggested they needed, and ... would not be able to go into retirement and keep helping the children financially ...

When I asked the couple why they kept sending money to their children, they gave me a response I have heard over and over in my career: "How can you NOT help out your children when they are in need?" I said I didn't know as my children were still underage and living at home, but surely there had to be a way to raise financially independent children.

So my curiosity got the best of me and I started to ask some questions about how they raised their children around money, in hopes that I might come closer to understanding what lessons to teach to make for an independent adult child.

I asked, "When your kids were little and living at home, what were your rules about buying things for them?"

They answered, "Well we grew up as children of parents who had lived during the Depression, and quite frankly felt very deprived growing up. So we just really wanted our children to have a different experience. I guess we sort of spoiled them, buying them most of the items they wanted as kids."

I asked, "Did you give them allowance, and if so, what did they use it for?"

They answered, "Yes, we gave them allowance, but it was their money to do with what they wanted. We had no rules for the use, nor do we really know where it went."

"So, you basically bought them whatever they wanted and gave them money to use however they chose, correct?" They replied in the affirmative.

I asked, "How about when they went to college? How did you work the finances then?"

They answered, "We paid the tuition, rent and set them up on a set amount monthly for food and some play money."

I asked, "Did they ever call home for more money, and if so, what did you do?"

They said, "Oh yes, probably every couple months, and what could we do? Of course we sent what they needed."

Lastly I asked, "Did they work in the summers between college semesters? If so, what was that money used for?"

They said, "Most of the time they did have summer work, but again, that money was theirs and we never questioned where they used it."

I told them it seemed quite obvious to me why these adult children were still attached to their parent's purse strings.

They'd never been taught anything about what it means to be financially independent. They had been given whatever they wanted, when they wanted it, no questions asked. Furthermore, they'd been led to believe that their parents were their bank account and their bailout plan for all their needs.

Now the truth of today's economy is that many adult children, even college graduates, are having a hard time finding work. Sometimes the best solution is for the kids to move home for a while.

When this is the case, expectations should be set concerning getting some type of work, contributing to some expenses, and of course household chores.

But in this family's story, this was not the case. Sadly, I've heard their story before, many times, and I've watched some retirees sabotage their own financial lives for the sake of adult children, especially when grandchildren are involved.

How do you cut off adult children who are still attached to you for financial support?

To begin with, I suggest a very open conversation with the adult children about how their financial situation is impeding your own desire to retire or _____(fill in the blank with your own unfulfilled dream). I'd truly like to believe that, in general, these kids would get the message and stop coming home for money. But just like a baby depends on its mother for nourishment, these children have maintained a dependence on their parents that they most likely don't know how to break.

In all honesty, I'm not sure how this couple resolved their situation, and for all I know they are still working at jobs they don't want to be at, at an age they deserve to be retired by. But the conversation should spark some great ideas for teaching young children and college age kids about financial independence from their parents. Did you glean any of them by reading this chapter?

Lessons Learned

1. Be cautious of the subliminal money messages you give to your children. They can lead to a dysfunctional relationship with money later in life.

2. Part of raising children is to teach them to be independent, both emotionally and financially.

3. Sometimes "tough love" can apply to money, too.

It's Just Money
So Why Does It Cause So Many Problems?

Because sometimes we think we are helping out, when in fact we are enabling dysfunctional or unsustainable behavior.

Chapter 10
When People Die

Of all the dysfunctions around money I have witnessed, some of the worst are those related to the death of a family member.

I've had adult children call me on the day of a parent's funeral—literally as they were leaving the church to get into their cars—to ask how soon they could get their share of the money. I've seen the other extreme, too, when we called beneficiaries months following a client's death to distribute their share of the estate, only to be told, "I don't want any of his damn money."

I don't think there is a person alive who doesn't have a story of family relationships destroyed over money squabbles following the death of a loved one. We've all heard about highly publicized wealthy estates where a family member is contesting a will, or about someone marrying into a wealthy family just for the chance to get named in a will.

> *I don't think there is a person alive who doesn't have a story of family relationships destroyed over money squabbles following the death of a loved one.*

You are probably familiar with the story of Anna Nicole Smith and her wealthy husband, old enough to be her grandfather. However, you don't need to be wealthy to fight over an estate; arguments over the deceased's money and belongings happen at all socioeconomic levels. The following stories are just a sampling of the countless problems that can arise around the death of a loved one.

Battling Over Inherited Money

A colleague of mine shared a story about a couple who had amassed several million dollars in investments, a house in an upscale neighborhood and a vacation home, both owned free and clear. His problem was the financial planning rule of thumb that all parental assets should be split evenly among the children, regardless of their individual financial situations. Although this unofficial rule can save a lot of heartache, some parents struggle with this decision when some children are far needier than the others.

This well-off couple had four grown children: three sons and one daughter. Two boys were married and had several children, but the third son was a consummate bachelor, although he had fathered a child out of wedlock. The two married sons were successful professionals who saved and planned for the future, but the bachelor son had made a habit of frivolously spending everything he ever earned despite earning a good salary.

The bachelor son also had relied heavily on his parents when he had custody of his child. He often called on them to babysit when he traveled for his job and to generally help parent his child, as he didn't have a spouse. His parents didn't mind this at all; in fact, although they had eleven grandchildren, they had developed a special affection for this one because of the enormous amount of time they had spent with him over the years.

Their only daughter was happily married to a minister of a very small church in a rural town some distance from where her parents lived. She had six children and didn't have the means to travel often to visit with her parents.

She had chosen to stay home in order to home school the children and to be actively involved in her husband's congregation. She led the youth ministry at the church and was loved and respected by all who knew her. Although she didn't get to see her parents often, and her children never got to know them very well, as the only daughter she was very emotionally tied to her mother. She talked to her mother on the phone several times a day.

On more than one occasion while visiting with their financial adviser, the well-off couple stressed over how to divide their estate when they died. They knew that two of their sons didn't need an inheritance because they had done so well for themselves. On the other hand, they were very critical of their third son's spending and inability to settle down, but they absolutely adored their special grandson and wanted to provide for him. They truly worried that with their son's spending habits, their grandchild would never see a dime of their inheritance. As for their daughter, clearly she needed the most help financially and had lived an admirable life of giving to others.

Their advisor repeatedly recommended a division of the estate into four equal parts, with the possibility of skipping the adults and leaving the inheritance in trust to the grandchildren. The clients also considered a trust for the grandchildren in which each would receive one-eleventh of the estate, but that would have greatly benefited their daughter, leaving over half of the estate to her children. The adviser tried to help them see that anything other than an even division of assets could surely cause fighting that could break up this family in the future.

The financial adviser also suggested that in favoring the bachelor son or the daughter, they were in fact penalizing the two sons who had made such good financial decisions all along. Any financial advisor or probate attorney who has been in business for any length of time can attest to the fighting that can occur over favoritism, especially when it is perceived that the other children had "dug their own ditch" so to speak, by their choices of careers, spending habits, or the number of children they chose to have.

In the end, this couple decided that they simply had to leave more for their daughter and their favorite grandson, so they left their main house outright to their daughter, and their less expensive vacation home in trust to their bachelor son's child. They split the money and investments evenly among all four adult children, all the time worrying that the spendthrift son would spend all the money before he even got to retirement.

Tragically, the couple died in a car accident when they were only in their sixties. But that was just the beginning of the problem. When the will was read, the explosions started. How dare the parents favor one grandchild over another, regardless of the circumstance! And as expected, the two professional sons felt completely slighted over getting none of the real estate, valued at over $1 million. The insults started flying between them and the bachelor brother over the bad financial decisions he had made over the years. The daughter very much tried to remain neutral—and why not: She was getting more than her siblings. At any rate, she simply wasn't a confrontational woman, nor was she really worried about money, either. She just wanted her parents back.

When the will was read, the explosions started. How dare the parents favor one grandchild over another, regardless of the circumstance! ... the two professional sons felt completely slighted ... The insults started flying between them ... The daughter ... just wanted her parents back.

In the end, the two professional sons contested the will. Although they ultimately lost, they dragged the settlement out for years, costing the estate over $300,000 in attorney's fees. They no longer speak to their younger brother. Although the sister is still in touch with them all, the son of the third brother has been ostracized by his ten first cousins and barely sees the rest of his extended family.

No matter what the circumstances may be, an even division of estates among all children is usually the recommended solution. The "rule of thumb" is almost always the best way. Still, a family meeting well in advance makes sense to discuss alternatives. At the very least, individual discussions with adult children might be warranted to see if any of the children are open to an uneven disposition of estates.

Lessons Learned

1. No matter how different their financial situations, grown children will almost always be hurt if their parents treat them differently in their will.

2. A discussion beforehand, so grown children will not be surprised when the will is read, will go a long way to resolving problems before they begin.

3. Sometimes a grandchild has to be protected from an irresponsible parent. In such cases, a trust can benefit a grandchild without disinheriting the parent.

It's Just Money
So Why Does It Cause So Many Problems?

Because money isn't just money. It can be a potent symbol of our relationships with our parents, children and siblings.

Battling Over Inherited Things

I knew of three siblings—two sisters and a brother—whose parents had recently died within a year of each other. The parents, Jim and Jenny, were of very modest means. They relied mostly on Social Security, although having lived through the Depression, that income was adequate for them. They had bought and paid off a two-bedroom, two-bath condominium on a lake in the Midwest, where they lived out their retirement. The bulk of their estate consisted of $60,000 in emergency savings and the residence, worth $90,000. As with most families, there were also lots of knick-knacks and belongings of great sentimental but little financial value.

All three adult children had done pretty well for themselves. Their parents made sure they all went to college and got a chance to make a good living. The oldest sister, Mary, was a nurse who had married a doctor and had two children. The younger sister, Joanie, was single and childless, with a great career as an account executive with a prominent ad agency. The baby brother, Steve, had become an engineer and married his high-school sweetheart, who stayed home full-time throughout their marriage to raise their children.

None of them desperately needed the $50,000 each would get from the estate, but problems occurred nonetheless, and always do when emotions are involved. For example, the daughters squabbled briefly over a family heirloom, a set of china handed down from their grandparents. They resolved the fight by splitting the set, each taking a set of six to keep in their home. What good is a place setting for six? But at least they were able to agree to that.

The big problem was the condo. All the children and grandchildren had visited there often and all had good memories. Mary and Steve had brought their children there for many a summer vacation to play in the lake and hang out with their grandparents. Both Mary and Steve wanted to keep the condominium, especially Steve, as he lived the closest and had spent the most time with his folks at the end of their lives. Going forward they were willing to share in the condo fees and upkeep in order to keep the home in the family.

Joanie, however, had been very busy building her career and hardly ever came to visit the condo. Her career had taken her far away from the Midwest to New York, and she never saw herself using the condo. She just wanted out.

In this case, Mom and Dad, like most parents, left their modest estate equally to their three adult children. That would give each child a one-third share of the lake condo, worth around $30,000 each, and one-third of the savings account, worth $20,000 each. But with Steve and Mary wanting to keep the condominium and Joanie wanting nothing to do with it, the burden fell on both Steve and Mary to buy out Joanie for her one-third of the condo, or pay her $15,000 each to even her up and make things equal. This didn't seem like a problem at first: Joanie would essentially end up with most of the savings account—$50,000— and Mary and Steve would each keep only $5,000 of the cash but own half of the condo.

After Mary discussed this with her husband, however, she came back to Steve and said that after further consideration, her husband felt that with two children in college far away from the Midwest, they really needed the extra cash, not the extra expenses of a second home. And he felt like they just wouldn't get any use out of the property. Being the logical man that he was, he felt sentiment was not a good enough reason to hold onto the house.

Sad as Mary was to let the condo go, she could see the wisdom in her husband's words, and had come to terms with it. Steve, however, was devastated. Under this arrangement, Steve would have to come up with a total of $60,000 to buy out both Mary and Joanie. He would only be receiving $20,000 of his parents' savings towards that amount. Steve had four children to put through college and had only a modest income as an engineer. His only option was to go out and borrow the money, which his own wife overruled.

Steve approached his sisters with the following offer: They would each keep a one-third share in the condo and they likewise would share its use, but he would pay all annual expenses and upkeep.

Sadly, neither sister would have anything to do with it. They didn't want the property and didn't understand why Steve felt so strongly about it. Steve was crushed. He was forced to list the property for sale, and he ultimately let his strongest emotional tie to his parents go. The saddest part of this story is that Steve no longer speaks to either of his sisters—over money, which interestingly, neither of the sisters needed, as they were both blessed financially.

> *Sadly, neither sister would have anything to do with it. They didn't want the property and didn't understand why Steve felt so strongly about it. Steve was crushed.*

I've often wondered if this situation would have been avoided. Could the parents have discussed the division of their small estate before they died, working out some arrangement that could make everyone happy?

Although hindsight is 20/20, I think if the parents had discussed their estate with their grown children beforehand, the situation could have turned out differently. If the three kids had had an open conversation with the financial data in front of them, they would have come to the conclusion that even though Steve and Mary wanted the lake house, there wouldn't be adequate money to buy out their other sibling.

Perhaps Steve and Mary would have chosen to buy a 2nd to die life insurance policy on their parents, with a death benefit big enough to buy out Joanie. If that wasn't an option due to cost of premiums or the insurability of their parents, Steve and Mary could have planned to save up additional money in advance so they could buy out their sister. If nothing else, the conversation might have allowed all parties to adjust to the fact that the property would ultimately have to be sold. Coming to this decision while the parents were still alive might have assuaged the emotional toll on the siblings, especially for Steve who was more emotionally connected to the lake house.

Lessons Learned

1. Conversations in advance about the "what if" scenarios we might face in life can always pave a smoother path for the potential reality in the future.

2. There are many solutions to problems if we address them before they exist.

3. We will never know where family stands on issues if we don't have open communication.

It's Just Money
So Why Does It Cause So Many Problems?

Because often our emotional connection to things has little to do with their actual financial value.

My Personal Reflections

Chapter 11
Disability Insurance

Just mention this type of insurance to a financial planning professional or insurance agent and watch them cringe. Why? Because this is by far one of the most difficult types of insurance to convince people they need to buy. It's the attitude that "it's never going to happen to me."

The statistics are staggering. It is estimated that one out of every eight people will suffer some type of disability lasting longer than 90 days at some point in their working lives. The statistic for how many people will die prematurely is significantly lower. Less than half of all companies carry short-term or long-term disability insurance for their employees. Yes, the Social Security Administration has benefits for people who are qualified for the insurance, but seven out of every ten people who apply for those disability benefits get turned down. Of those who could qualify, the maximum payment per month is only around $2,000 a month.

The possibility of being out of work due to sickness or accident and the devastation that this could bring to one's financial plan is astounding. From a financial viewpoint, it can be worse than death. If you die, you are gone, no longer requiring food, shelter and clothes. If you are disabled, not only do you still need life's basic necessities, you may require additional care or help in your life. Despite the logic, when I've advised clients to buy this insurance or supplement their group coverage, these are some of the objections I've heard:

"Funny, I don't know anyone who's ever been disabled."

"I can't imagine any type of disability that could prevent me from doing my work, since I earn money just using my brain, mouth, computer, etc."

My personal favorite: "If something like that happened to me, I'd just kill myself!"

I think there is a basic lack of understanding about what disability insurance actually does for you. I've heard clients say, "Well my medical insurance would cover that." To avoid confusion, I think we should change the name from "disability," which sounds vaguely medical, to "income replacement" insurance.

> *... there is a basic lack of understanding about what disability insurance actually does for you. ... I think we should change the name to "income replacement" insurance.*

Even I fell victim to this lack of understanding. At the age of 23, when leaving my position with an architecture firm to move to Chicago, I was offered the opportunity to maintain the group disability coverage for the low cost of $16 a month. I said "no thanks" because I was sure my next company would have it. It wasn't until I went into financial planning two years later that I realized that the policy that had been offered to me was disability (income replacement) insurance, not health insurance, and the new firm in Chicago hadn't even offered it. It was at that point that I bought my first disability insurance policy, one that I still pay for today. I pray that I waste all those premiums dollars and never collect, but as we know, bad things do happen.

Read on and see if you don't become convinced that disability insurance is a "must" for any financially responsible worker.

The #1 Insurance Policy Every Working Person Needs

Many years ago, I met an incredible woman named Connie. She was self-employed as a freelance journalist, married, with one small child. The thing I loved about Connie was that she was quite sophisticated about money even though she was only in her late 20's. Connie and her husband had just had the baby and she wanted to make sure she had all her ducks in a row now that they had a child. She had done her planning well on her own, but the responsibility of having a child made her reach out for an outside opinion from a financial planning professional.

She and her husband had a very modest income, and lived in a small house in town that was easy to afford. To me, the most amazing thing about Connie's financial planning was that she had already bought disability insurance before she had even met me. I am usually the first person who brings this up to people, and I can't tell you how many insist that it will never happen to them, and don't go forward with my recommendation to purchase this coverage. Connie simply knew that being self-employed she had to take care of herself and purchase the benefits that so many people rely on their companies to provide.

When she explained what she was doing, it seemed that the only thing lacking was life insurance. The preferable type of life insurance is permanent coverage, although many a pundit will debate that there are better uses of one's money. The thing that makes it preferable is that it is *permanent,* whereas term insurance is *temporary.* Be that as it may, permanent policies are more expensive, so Connie and her husband bought a combination of term and permanent coverage to cover their needs.

Not two years later, Connie called me with some devastating news. Following a routine checkup, Connie had been diagnosed with a rare type of cancer in her pelvic bone. When she first told me of the diagnosis, she immediately stated how happy she was that she bought all that life insurance when she did. She knew she might not ever be able to buy life insurance ever again. I was amazed that her mind even considered that thought at this trying time in her life.

Connie's treatment started immediately with surgery, which was enormously invasive, carving out portions of her pelvic bone and surrounding tissues, including her buttocks. This was followed by five weeks of radiation and then a second surgery.

Fortunately, the surgeons felt they had gotten all of the malignancy, but Connie was left in a lot of physical pain. In addition, the surgery left her unable to sit down comfortably for any period of time, which was essential to her work as a journalist.

Needless to say, Connie couldn't work. She applied for disability insurance through the Social Security Administration and filed a claim for the personal disability coverage she had been so wise to buy at such a young age. Between those two sources of disability income, and her husband's salary, they have been able to stay in their home and even continue to save for the future.

... Connie couldn't work. She applied for disability insurance through the Social Security Administration and filed a claim for the personal disability coverage she had been so wise to buy at such a young age. ... they have been able to stay in their home and even continue to save for the future.

This story has a lot of happy endings to it…

1) Connie had been told that the surgeries may have made her unable to have more children, but two years later she gave birth to another healthy baby.

2) The original term life insurance that Connie purchased—annual renewable term—had become quite expensive. But ten years after being declared cancer-free, she was able to get underwriting for new life insurance, at a standard issue rate, and replace the old expensive coverage.

Two times now, the insurance company paying the disability claims has offered her a lump sum "pay off" so they could stop paying her monthly. At first glance, it seemed hard to turn down. The company was offering a one-time payment of $250,000. But true to her nature, instead of just grabbing the quarter-million dollars, Connie called me immediately to ask for my input.

Doing some simple math, we calculated that the lump sum covered about eight years of monthly payments—nine years if the lump sum were invested and earned interest while she was drawing her monthly paycheck. The first time this offer was made, Connie was 39 years old. She knew she would never work as a journalist again, making her eligible for the disability income monthly check until age 65.

Together we decided that she shouldn't take the lump-sum offer. It seemed to benefit the insurance company more than it benefited Connie.

This is another example of, "it will never happen to me." But it does happen to someone; how do you know it won't be you?

Lessons Learned

1. Research insurance and buy it when you're young, even if you don't have a lot of money, because you never know when you will need it. This is especially true if you have dependent children.

2. Consider your options rationally, not emotionally. In this case, $250,000 looked like a great deal of money, but after Connie crunched the numbers, it wasn't so much after all.

It's Just Money
So Why Does It Cause So Many Problems?

Because when you are young, it is difficult to plan for potential disaster, especially at a time when you are feeling invincible.

The Amazing Dr. Dave and What We Can Learn from his Ordeal

Dave's parents were very proud when he told them he was going to be a doctor. His father never finished high school because he had to go to work. He owned a service station, and with the help of his wife who was a nurse, the family never went without, although they were far from rich. Still, Dave and his siblings were determined to make it and they all became successful.

Because becoming a doctor is a long journey involving a pre-med course of study at college, four years of medical school, internship and residency, Dave was 33 years old when he finally got his first decent paying job. He started out earning $105,000 and felt like this was a huge amount of money. And it was for him. He was single, with no kids, and had been brought up by a frugal father who would turn out all the lights in the house early in the evening, to save energy. Dave learned early in life not to be very materialistic, so this salary was more than enough for him.

In fact, Dave felt rich and thought that now was the time to do what rich people do, which in his mind was to buy life insurance. So Dave got a referral to an insurance agent and went in for an appointment, where he had an interesting discussion. As he had no dependents, the agent said he had minimal, if no need for life insurance—but definitely had a great need for disability insurance (which, as I said in the last chapter, should more aptly be named "income replacement insurance").

The agent explained that Dave had a far greater chance of becoming disabled over the next 20 years than dying, and recommended Dave buy the maximum coverage the insurance company would write on him. So Dave, being the smart, rich guy that he was, did just that, even though the premiums seemed very high.

Over the years, the insurance agent sent Dave notices suggesting that he increase the coverage if his income had gone up. Dave responded every other year or so, made the appointment and increased his coverage to the maximums allowed at those times. Eventually, he was earning more than half a million dollars a year.

The agent explained that Dave had a far greater chance of becoming disabled over the next 20 years than dying, and recommended Dave buy the maximum coverage ... So Dave, being the smart, rich guy that he was, did just that, even though the premiums seemed very high.

When he was 43 years old and still unmarried, Dave happened to have his girlfriend over on a Sunday night. Sometime during the night, she was awakened by a big *thump.* She got out of bed to find Dave lying face down on the bathroom floor, barely able to speak but whispering, "I can't breathe." She called 911, then turned him over and started doing mouth-to-mouth breathing until the paramedics arrived.

Dave had gotten up in the middle of the night to use the bathroom and must have tripped over something, falling face forward on the floor. No, he had not been drinking, and no, he was not overweight; in fact, he was a healthy, fit man. Four days later at the hospital, Dave awoke from his coma to learn that he had broken two vertebrae in his neck and was on a ventilator. The only good news was that the spinal cord injury was "incomplete," so there was some potential for regeneration, but no promises.

He was on the ventilator for fourteen days and underwent surgery on his neck, following which he was transferred to Atlanta's Shepherd Spinal Center, a renowned clinic for spinal cord and brain injuries. He was there for two months, lying flat on his back, only able to move his eyes back and forth and speak in a whisper. Pretty scary.

He was then sent home, fully paralyzed from the neck down, and his medical plan, although excellent, covered only a limited period at a day program at Shepherd. It was up to him to figure out how to get there every day. He couldn't even get himself in and out of a vehicle, even if he could find someone to drive him there daily.

This is where the disability insurance comes into play. After the waiting period was complete, Dave started to receive a check for $10,000 a month, free of tax, as it had been an individual policy not a group plan. That would seem like plenty of money to live on, and certainly was enough to pay his monthly bills. But here's the stuff that no one thinks about. Dave was paralyzed and confined to a wheelchair. He couldn't feed, dress, nor undress himself, or maneuver himself from the wheelchair to his bed. Dave needed full-time care in his home.

Medical insurance does not cover this (long-term care insurance would, but you rarely find a 40-year-old who owns this kind of insurance.) Being diligent and careful, Dave found capable caregivers for only $10 an hour, almost half the cost of going through a service. Even with that, he is currently spending $4,400 a month on in-home care. That $10,000 monthly disability check is getting squeezed pretty thin!

Two years after his accident, Dave realized that the twenty outpatient physical therapy visits per year that are covered by his medical insurance plan were not producing any results. So he sought physical therapy through an elite provider not covered by medical insurance. After six months of this high-end therapy, Dave had made so much progress that he decided he would continue this therapy until he no longer experiences any improvement, runs out of money or dies. The therapy is costing him $1,000 a week … that's $52,000 a year. In addition, in order to get out and about, Dave had to spend $55,000 to purchase a minivan retrofitted for wheelchair access. Insurance doesn't cover that either.

Amazingly, I recently went out to lunch with Dave. Although he can't drive, he can maneuver himself in and out of the van, into the restaurant and up to his table, eat by himself and enjoy a glass of wine with me. He can now bend fully from the waist to his lap, and with assistance, can get out of his chair and walk with one forearm cane and someone on the other side. It is truly a miracle and a testament to the enduring spirit and strength of a human being.

Lessons Learned

1. Yes it can happen to you. Buy the necessary disability insurance regardless of the cost. And never cancel it, even during tough financial times. Dave's recovery probably wouldn't have been possible without his excellent coverage.

2. By living beneath his means during those previous ten years, Dave was able to foot the bill for the therapy that will most likely allow this brilliant and super-motivated human being to one day walk and work again.

It's Just Money
So Why Does It Cause So Many Problems?

One cause: Many people don't think about managing risk. They are in denial, thinking "it won't happen to me."

Chapter 12
Death and Life Insurance

Ben Franklin once said, "Everything appears to promise that will last, but in this world nothing is certain but death and taxes." But we don't know the when and how of death.

I love to ask my clients this trick question: "What is the most common cause of death?"

Typical responses are "heart attack" or "cancer." While these are common causes, statistically, in the United States, you're going to live to a ripe old age. It would seem then that life insurance isn't entirely necessary; we won't collect until it isn't needed anymore. However, we of course need it in case death is premature. That's the thing about any kind of insurance: you buy it, and then pray it never happens.

That's a better alternative than simply hoping you never need it, although many choose that route, as dangerous as it is. That's why we have laws that require us to insure our cars, and why mortgage companies usually insist we keep insurance on our homes. But I have found through my work as a financial planner that people often debate the value of life insurance, which is not mandated. "Do I really need it? I hate to be worth more dead than alive," they ask themselves. And my personal favorite excuse, "She'll just find some rich dude to marry if I die."

Yet out of all the insurance that we contemplate buying, it's the one insurance contract that we *know* will pay off, because we *will* die one day. It's ironic that more people probably buy the extended warranty on their new flat screen TV (yes, they call it a warranty, but it's really insurance) than carry the correct amount of life insurance to protect their family in the unfortunate case of premature death, and subsequent loss of income.

This next chapter covers both the value of financial planning for people of any income, and the saving grace of life insurance.

It's ironic that more people probably buy the extended warranty on their new flat screen TV (yes, they call it a warranty, but it's really insurance) than carry the correct amount of life insurance to protect their family in the unfortunate case of premature deat ...

Will You be Able to Keep the House if your Spouse Dies?

I hired Wanda to work for me as my fulltime assistant in 1997, just three months after the birth of my second child.

Since this story is about Wanda and her situation, you need to know that she was not blessed by being born into a wealthy, highly educated family. These were people who had to choose to work versus go to college. She was raised in a small town in western Kentucky. Following the divorce of her parents, her father and grandmother raised her. Wanda married shortly after high school and had two children. The marriage didn't work out, but Wanda eventually recovered from that difficult situation and married Bill.

Having known Bill for some time now, I can tell you Wanda struck gold. Bill and Wanda raised her two children, and helped to raise Bill's two children from his first marriage, who lived with his ex-wife. Eventually, Wanda came to work for me.

I explained to her when she started that one of the things I expected my assistant to do for me was to enter each new client's financial data into our financial planning software. I suggested that the best way for her to learn this software program was to enter her own data and run a financial plan for herself and Bill.

Wanda told Bill they needed to fill out this worksheet on their financial data so she could learn the software and, as a side benefit, they would get a financial plan. Over the next few months, I repeatedly asked Wanda, "Where is that worksheet?" and the answer was, "Bill is working on it." At year-end, I stopped asking, figuring there was something else going on and it was probably none of my business. Wanda mastered the financial software using other new client data.

It was about a year-and-a-half later that Wanda brought in her worksheet and told me that Bill was ready to have me review their finances. She explained that he had been reluctant to complete the form and start the process because he believed that financial planners only work with "rich people" and they were far from rich. Furthermore, he didn't want to waste my time, or feel like they were a charity case as I couldn't make any money off their plan.

First of all, *everyone* can benefit by having a financial professional review his or her situation. Unless financial planning is your area of expertise, a new set of eyes looking over your situation can often reveal areas that can be improved. In addition, I would have helped them, or any friend, for free because I believe in what I do and I loved them and wanted to help. There is always someone out there who can give you good advice. You can always find an independent financial planner and pay an hourly rate, or even a commission-based advisor who is somewhat new in the industry that will do a financial plan for a reasonable fee.

> *... everyone can benefit by having a financial professional review his or her situation. Unless financial planning is your area of expertise, a new set of eyes looking over your situation can often reveal areas that can be improved.*

As I read the worksheet, I found that I could, indeed, help them. Bill earned $45,000 a year and Wanda earned $30,000. They owned their own home, which was worth around $125,000, and they had only $25,000 left on the mortgage. They had purchased it with money Bill had inherited from his mother, making a substantial down payment to keep their mortgage payments relatively low.

They had a bit in savings through Bill's 401(k) and small pension plan, and some of Bill's inheritance invested in mutual funds—a total of $150,000.

For life insurance, Bill had a death benefit face policy value of twice his pay through work—about $90,000—and a very small whole life policy that he'd had for years. It would pay around $40,000 if he died and had built up some decent cash value over the years. Wanda had no life insurance.

Unfortunately, they had around $20,000 in credit card debt, about which they were quite embarrassed.

The financial plan was simple to create and Bill and Wanda were exceptionally easy to work with, doing everything I suggested. They refinanced the house and wrapped the consumer debt into the mortgage. This reduced the overall monthly payment to one-third of what they had been paying, allowing them to increase savings.

The next thing we addressed was the life insurance. The plan showed that Bill was clearly underinsured. We used the cash value of his small life insurance policy to buy a $150,000 permanent policy without increasing his premiums. We then bought an additional $250,000 of term life to bring his total insurance coverage, including the group insurance, to $490,000, just over 10 times his income. We also bought a term life policy on Wanda.

All parties felt good about the interaction. Bill was pleased and wondered why he had waited so long to come in and discuss the plan. Wanda was proud of her husband and her boss. My reward was the good feelings that came from having helped them.

Then one day Wanda told me that Bill had a headache that just wouldn't go away. We pondered that it was the darn allergies that plague many in the Southeast. But after 10 days of the headache, Bill's doctor ordered a CT scan—which revealed a golf ball-sized brain tumor. Bill had emergency surgery, followed by six weeks of radiation treatments. The prognosis was not good.

Wanda had to be there for Bill, but my job was to focus on their finances. The first thing I did was review their financial plan, running the numbers with the insurance proceeds paying out and eliminating Bill's income. The analysis confirmed that the insurance was adequate.

Sadly the tumor returned and Bill's condition deteriorated. Friends and family gathered, knowing the end was near. At one point, I called the house and talked to a friend from church. I told her who I was and that I needed her to relay a message to Bill from me. I said, "Tell him Karen called and she wants you to know that she has checked your financial plan with the life insurance proceeds, and that Wanda is going to be just fine. He doesn't need to worry ... Karen will take care of her."

At the funeral, the church friend told me that she had whispered in Bill's ear what I had said. She said his expression had immediately relaxed and eased up. Within thirty minutes of my call, Bill had passed on.

At the funeral, Wanda came to me, dazed and in a fog. She said, "Karen, everyone keeps asking me if I'll be able to keep the house. I don't know what to say. Will I be able to keep the house?" I put my arms around her and said, "Of course, you will be able to keep the house."

Financial planning makes things like this possible.

Lessons Learned

1. Financial planning is for everyone, not just the wealthy.

2. Insurance and debt planning do not have to be expensive or time-consuming, but the penalties for failing to make a plan could be devastating.

It's Just Money
So Why Does It Cause So Many Problems?

One cause: As we go through life, sometimes the unexpected happens, and it's not always something good … plan for the worst and hope and pray for the best.

Who's Going To Die First— and What If You're Wrong?

One of the more bizarre conversations that financial advisors have with their clients is about life expectancy. I always ask clients how long they think they will live. In order to run a retirement analysis we have to pick what is know as an "expiration date." I like to use age 95 or even older; because some people do live that long and it would be tragic to run out of money at that late age.

This story is about a conversation with clients around planning for death, and how sometimes we simply get it wrong.

Sissy and Fred, parents of dear friends of mine, were that perfect retired older couple. Incredibly hip and physically fit, they loved to travel and were great fun to be around. When I met them, Sissy was 71 and Fred was 76, and they were seeking financial advice for the small amount of savings they had. They both had pensions from work and, along with their Social Security, they had enough to live on. They were already retired when they came to me for help. Their income sources were as follows:

- Social Security – Fred = $860 month

- Social Security – Sissy= $950 month

- Pension – Fred = $880 month

- Pension – Sissy = $1,865 month

That totaled almost $55,000 a year in fixed income. They were also using about $20,000 a year from savings and investments. They had approximately $300,000 in

IRAs and $65,000 in savings. They also owned their home outright.

Their goals were quite modest. They simply wanted to travel more, buy a new car in two to five years and basically grow their investments so they could leave something for their two grown children.

Fred and Sissy were "Depression Babies." They were born in 1924 and 1929, and they had similar attitudes about money. In short, they could pinch a penny tighter than most. This is the generation of people that learned to live a certain way thanks to the Great Depression. They reused aluminum foil, kept all bags for future use and saved bones from any meat to make soup. Financial advisors like working with this group because our number one goal is to make sure clients don't run out of money.

This is the generation of people that learned to live a certain way thanks to the Great Depression. ... Financial advisors like working with this group because our number one goal is to make sure clients don't run out of money.

However, even with prudent savers, life can get complicated. Both Sissy and Fred had been schoolteachers most of their lives; as a result, they had generous pensions. (Teachers and government workers generally are among some of the last employees to have companies provide them with pensions.)

Pension plans, also known as "defined benefit plans", typically offer a variety of payout alternatives from which the retiree chooses one upon retirement, and these decisions are usually irrevocable. Sometimes the payout options include a lump sum, but in many cases you will get only monthly annuity payments as options. The highest payment a person could receive, called 100 percent straight life, will pay for the pension owner's life only and end at the owner's death. Another option, paying a lower amount, would pay the pension owner's spouse a percentage of the owner's annuity for the spouse's lifetime. The higher the percentage the surviving spouse is guaranteed, the lower the initial monthly payment to the retiree will be.

For Sissy and Fred the decision seemed simple. Sissy was five years younger than Fred and statistically women have longer life expectancies than men. More importantly, Fred had several medical conditions including an active aneurysm, and he had had some heart troubles in his mid 40's. Sissy, on the other hand, was very healthy.

When they came to see me they were already drawing on their pensions. The payout decisions they had made were sensible given their situation. They assumed Sissy would outlive Fred, so they took 100 percent straight life on her, meaning Fred would get zero if she died. They took the lowest payout possible on Fred, giving Sissy a 100 percent ongoing payment on Fred's pension if he died first as expected. It's true that Sissy's pension was more than double Fred's, but the planning made sense.

Unfortunately life rarely works out as we plan it will. When Sissy turned 72, she was diagnosed with acute myelogenous leukemia, a rare form of blood cancer, which is treatable, but ultimately fatal. She lived only two more years. Fred is still alive at 86, defying all odds and getting ready to sell the original house and move into a retirement community.

Here's the financial predicament they created by incorrectly "guessing" who would die first. As a married couple the fixed income came to $4,555 a month. After Sissy died, Fred would get his pension and Sissy's Social Security, since it was the higher of the two, coming to a monthly income of only $1,830. If they had made other assumptions, Fred could have maintained a monthly income of around $2,815 a month—still a decline, but not nearly as drastic.

Fortunately, Fred's frugal nature has seen him through. His expenses are only $1,200 a month. His house has appreciated to almost $500,000 and his combined savings, even after eight years of mandatory withdrawals from his IRAs, still total around $325,000. Of course the retirement community he's moving into will be costly, but he can afford it. And it looks like he'll still achieve his and Sissy's dream of leaving an inheritance to their two children.

Lessons Learned

1. Prudent planning goes a long way to making financial dreams come true, but it is impossible to predict every eventuality.

2. With all statistics, there are also exceptions.

3. Even when bad luck foils your plans, a frugal nature can still overcome many obstacles.

It's Just Money
So Why Does It Cause So Many Problems?

Because we can only deal with possibilities and probabilities—not certainties.

Why People Don't Buy Life Insurance—and the Problem with Waiting

Life insurance should be the easiest insurance sale on the planet. All other types of insurance are a gamble that you hope never pay off. But with life insurance, death is a certainty.

One of the greatest debates in the insurance world is whether people should buy permanent insurance (whole life, universal life, variable life), or term life. Permanent life insurance should last your entire life and provide coverage as long as you need it, as long as you pay the proposed premiums and the policy performs as illustrated. You can also cash it out earlier for a return of some premium, should you decide you no longer need it. Some advisors recommend term insurance, which is basically temporary coverage, primarily to insure against premature death versus old age. These advisors suggest that you can invest the money saved by not paying the higher premium for permanent insurance and do better financially.

There's no correct answer to this debate, and trusting that you will reach age 60 or 65 and no longer need life insurance is really another type of gamble. Only permanent life insurance gives you that option. We could also argue about whether people would have the discipline to invest those premium dollars elsewhere, but that is not the point of this conversation.

It goes without saying that if you have anyone who depends on you financially for support—spouse, children, parents—you need life insurance coverage if you want to be sure they are taken care of in case you die.

Nevertheless, I'm continually flabbergasted by the many reasons people have for not buying life insurance, or postponing the decision.

I once met a couple when they came to my office to discuss the transfer of a late parent's account to them. I described my full services as a financial planner. They both immediately saw the value of the described services and certainly wanted to use all of the services that my firm could offer.

The husband, John, was a dentist with his own practice, which allowed his wife to stay home and raise their three children, ages 11, 8 and 6.

Like so many young and self-employed people, John had spent a decade building up his practice and scraping by in the early years. As his income grew and his practice became profitable, he spent a large proportion of the profits, moving to a nicer office, hiring more staff, and upgrading his family's home and cars. Of course everyone deserves to enjoy the fruits of their labor, but it was time for John to take a step back and evaluate his entire financial plan.

In the push to grow his practice, John had reached the age of 36 with no disability insurance, life insurance or retirement plan in place. I told John and his wife Judy that time was of the essence for moving forward with all of these necessary components to their financial plan. His family would suffer if he were to die or become disabled, as they would have no means of financial support. And the earlier retirement savings could begin, the more valuable those investments would be over time. Both he and Judy agreed wholeheartedly.

As you may know, to qualify for life insurance, you must prove that you are healthy. You are also required to disclose specifics about your health and habits, as well as your hobbies. Your answers to the questions affect how you will be underwritten by the insurance company. If you are very healthy, you might get "Preferred" status, which is even better than "Standard" status. Standard means you are of average health for a person of your age, whereas "Preferred" means your health is better than average and so you will be priced out as a younger person.

On the other hand, certain health factors can have a negative impact, such as weight, cholesterol levels, and blood pressure, causing you to be "Rated," or priced out as an older person. Your choice of hobbies, like parachuting, flying an airplane and hang gliding, might lead to exclusions of death benefits. Last but not least is the dreaded cigarette smoker rating, which can double the required premiums for life insurance coverage.

John and Judy were non-smokers and in pretty good health, although they both were quite heavy. I suggested that before we requested quotes for the rates, we should attempt to predetermine their underwriting classification. Basically, I had to tell this couple that it appeared they would get rated for their height-to-weight ratios.

They said they'd have to think about it and get back to me. When they called back, they excitedly shared that they had both started diets, joined a gym, and would call me once they fell into the weight range for standard rates. I never heard back from this couple, nor did I expect to. I have seen people wait more than twenty years to quit smoking, and they still haven't bought the appropriate life insurance. I have seen countless others postpone the

I always suggest to either the smoker who intends to quit, or the overweight person who's planning to diet, that it is wiser to buy the insurance with the more expensive premiums than to risk being uninsured. ... the insured person can reapply for a premium modification.

decision to purchase life insurance for any number of reasons rather than doing the right thing immediately.

I always suggest to either the smoker who intends to quit, or the overweight person who's planning to diet, that it is wiser to buy the insurance with the more expensive premiums than to risk being uninsured. Once the habit has been given up or the weight lost, the insured person can reapply for a premium modification. Sadly, too many people still choose to wait.

Unfortunately, death or disability are quite random in striking at any time; neither do they give you notice.

Lessons Learned

1. There are many things you can cut back on if money is tight. Proper life insurance isn't one of them —it's essential if anyone depends on you.

2. Don't wait until you are in a better position to buy life insurance; you never know when you'll need it.

It's Just Money
So Why Does It Cause So Many Problems?

Because the prospect of our deaths can be so hard to face, we end up not thinking about how our loved ones will fare financially without us.

My Personal Reflections

Chapter 13
Long-Term Care Insurance

When I went into the financial service business 23 years ago, long-term care (LTC) insurance was virtually unknown as a risk management insurance vehicle. Some companies were underwriting it as far back as thirty years ago, but it has only been in the last decade that LTC insurance has become commonly known.

Its purpose is to help offset the costs of care for someone with a long-term illness, which is often, but not always, due to old age. LTC insurance may cover such care whether it's in one's home or in a nursing home facility. Virtually everyone knows of a family where a parent or grandparent had to have extended care and how incredibly expensive it can be. Currently, the average cost for a full-time nursing home facility in the United States is over $53,000 a year, and considerably more in certain parts of the country.

Although Medicaid can provide coverage, you have to deplete most of your assets in order to qualify for it. In the case of a single person, that means no potential inheritance for heirs, and for a married couple, it could mean financial devastation for the healthy spouse.

For a single person, you can't qualify for Medicaid unless you have less than $2,000 in "countable" assets.

Although Medicaid can provide coverage, you have to deplete most of your assets in order to qualify for it. In the case of a single person, that means no potential inheritance for heirs, and for a married couple, it could mean financial devastation for the healthy spouse.

For a married couple, the healthy spouse is eligible for ½ the joint assets, but no more than $109,560 (for 2010) in addition to "non-countable" assets*

The solution is an LTC policy, and it is vitally important to understand it and consider the issues. Indeed, with people living longer than ever before and saving less than in prior decades, an LTC plan can help a family avoid a financial disaster.

*non countable assets include things like personal possessions, 1 car, a house as long as it has less than $500K in equity, for example.

Gambling with Your Future: The Long-term Care Dilemma

I have always practiced what I preach, so at only 43 years old, I bought Long Term Care policies for my husband and myself.

In 2008, three years later, my family income was rapidly reducing due to market declines on my clients' accounts; in addition, my husband was in the midst of pursing his dream to become a teacher. In the middle of this, my long-term care insurance premium came due. I had chosen to pay this bill annually as it was less expensive that way.

I had a typical human reaction to the several thousand dollar bill ... UGH! "Maybe I should just cancel this insurance", I thought. "I could always buy it later when things are better for us financially". (It didn't help that the bill arrived around the holidays.) Instead I made the decision to pay it that year, but to cancel in 2009 if things hadn't improved by then.

I had a typical human reaction to the several thousand dollar bill ... UGH! "Maybe I should just cancel this insurance", I thought. "I could always buy it later when things are better for us financially".

Time went by and things got significantly worse financially before they turned around. I was having lunch with a girlfriend and we were sharing stories about events in our lives and other friends' lives as well. My friend was particularly sad that day, because of a conversation she'd had with a cousin the previous night.

This cousin and his wife had married when they were both in their mid-twenties. They had several children, and the wife stayed home to raise the kids while the husband worked in the banking industry. They bought a house, started saving for retirement and building up college saving accounts for their children.

But following the birth of their last child, the wife was diagnosed with ALS, also known as Lou Gehrig's disease. This disease is a death sentence, as there is no known cure. The average life expectancy is around five years, with a slow decline in physical abilities.

My girlfriend was sharing with me how hard her cousin's life had become. For whatever reason, his wife had lived more than 10 years, which in some ways was a blessing, but financially her longevity was a curse. The state program for Medicaid covered only eight hours a day of in-home care. With several children to get out the door each day and a 45-minute commute each way to work, her cousin could only work about six hours a day at the office. His employer was being incredibly gracious in letting him keep his job, but even with that, the financial toll on the family was huge.

Eventually, the cousin and his wife and children lost their home, declared bankruptcy and didn't have a cent to their names. None of the children had even graduated high school yet, so college was looming.

I listened to this devastating story and reflected back on my own desire to drop my personal long-term care insurance due to "tough times." It goes without saying that when that bill came around the following December, and financially things were just a little better than the year before, I didn't think twice about renewing the coverage.

As with all insurance purchases, do your research and make sure you buy from a reputable company that has a history of paying claims.

Lessons Learned

1. Don't gamble. The stakes are too high to merit a bet that major problems won't crop up. Pay the insurance bill when it's due.

2. Think long term. A major insurance bill may seem like a steep price when times are tough, but you can always squeeze a few extra dollars out of the budget. You won't be able to do that when disaster strikes.

It's Just Money
So Why Does It Cause So Many Problems?

One cause: We're guilty of short-term thinking when it comes to potential long-term problems.

Should You Buy Long-Term Care Insurance For Parents?

Many years ago a couple, "Jack and Jill," approached me saying they wanted to buy LTC insurance for all four of their parents, who were in their mid to late 60s.

Jack and Jill had done a pretty good job so far in their personal financial planning. Good savers, they had put away money for their children's college educations. They had good paying jobs, lived within their means and looked forward to retiring in the next fifteen to twenty years.

Their parents were fine financially, but certainly not wealthy. Jack and Jill had a few siblings each, but they were the most financially successful of all the adult children. They knew that if anything were to happen to one of the parents, it would most certainly fall on their shoulders to help out financially. And although they had good jobs and money put away, they couldn't bankroll an extended stay in a nursing home.

I told the couple that their thinking was right on track, and that even though the cost of the insurance would eat into their ability to save, they should look into LTC because their parents couldn't afford to pay for it themselves.

I started to collect the data I needed to run quotes for the parents. As is normal with most people in their mid to late sixties, the parents had a few medical issues, but were fully self-functioning and living independently. One parent had had colon cancer, but had been cancer-free for more than seven years. Another had had some heart issues that required angioplasty and stents about five years previously, but had not had a heart attack. There was one serious concern: one of the parents had just been diagnosed with the earliest stages of dementia.

We took all four of the parents' applications and submitted them to multiple insurance companies for underwriting. LTC insurance was still new then and advisors didn't have a lot of experience with how it worked, so I was shocked when three of the four applications were turned down. The parents with the heart and cancer issues were told they could eventually get insurance in the future, as more time elapsed without reoccurrences. LTC insurance premiums, however, are based on the age you are when you buy the policy, and the cost was already almost beyond what Jack and Jill could afford to pay. Years later it would be unaffordable, and the parents might have even more medical issues by then.

Jack and Jill made the decision to buy the insurance for the one parent who could qualify and instead to buy the insurance for themselves. I was surprised by that decision, as at that point insurance professionals were reaching out to people in their late fifties and early sixties for LTC policies, and this couple was in their mid forties.

... I took it upon myself to run some calculations on the benefits of buying LTC insurance at age 40 versus age 50. I would have guessed that it was better to wait until age 50, because even though the cost would be higher ... But my calculations proved me wrong ...

Over the next few years, I took it upon myself to run some calculations on the benefits of buying LTC insurance at age 40 versus age 50. I would have guessed that it was better to wait until age 50, because even though the cost would be higher, you would have saved on a decade's worth of premiums. But my calculations proved me wrong: It actually made sense to buy the insurance at age 40 and pay those extra ten years. In other words, if you bought the policy at 50 and lived to at least 67, from that point on your total premiums would be have added up to more money than if you had started at age 40.

I made a few immediate changes in my financial planning practice—and in my own life. First of all, I bought long-term care insurance for both my husband and myself. We were in our early forties. I then started to bring up the subject of long-term care coverage to all my clients who were 40 and older. Not all of them chose to purchase it, but at least I'm educating them on their options.

Three years later, I got a call from Jill. She hadn't been feeling so great lately—tired and sluggish—so she had gone to the doctor for a full physical. Many appointments and tests later, Jill was diagnosed with leukemia. Her prognosis was excellent, and it was highly likely she would survive and be cured. She was calling to find out whether her policy would cover the cost of a caregiver in her home, should her condition require it. Her concern was that her husband really needed to continue at his job to pay the monthly bills, because her income was going away for an unknown period of time.

The answer was of *course her* policy would cover that; that's exactly what it was designed to do. As it turns out, Jill didn't need to make a claim, as her treatments did not incapacitate her. But what struck me was that now Jill was just like one of the three parents who originally got turned down for the insurance when they wanted to buy it: She was now uninsurable! If they hadn't decided to buy the insurance when they did, in their forties, she most likely would never qualify or if she did, the price would be unaffordable because she would be so much older.

Once again, so much of financial planning is for planning for the unknowns of the future. Who would have ever thought?

Lessons Learned

1. Plan ahead. We all know we're going to die, so we have life insurance, but we don't plan to be incapacitated. You have to think about all the possibilities.

2. Think rationally, not emotionally. When you're 40, old age seems so far away and you think there's plenty of time to buy LTC insurance. But you may actually save money by buying it earlier.

It's Just Money
So Why Does It Cause So Many Problems?

Many people don't think about future problems nor do they do the math to determine the better buy. It's easier to just plow ahead and hope things work out for the best.

My Personal Reflections

Chapter 14
Investing and Diversification

Diversification means different things to different people, and it's an important concept in creating an investment portfolio. Diversification can be thought of as spreading your investment dollars into various asset classes to add balance to your portfolio. Although it doesn't guarantee a profit, it may be able to reduce the volatility of your portfolio. Yet most folks agree that the word implies, "Don't put all your eggs in one basket." Other interpretations include "don't have all your investments with one investment advisor" (which I don't agree with, as a good advisor would have you appropriately diversified with different money managers or fund companies), or "don't have all your investments in one fund company."

One of the biggest investment mistakes people tend to make is keeping too much money in one particular company's stock. In many cases this occurs because the investor works for the company and perhaps receives the company stock as a bonus or incentive or even as a match inside a 401(k).

Although companies generally allow the employee to diversify out of the company stock over time, many people choose to stay with the company stock for a variety of

> *One of the biggest investment mistakes people tend to make is keeping too much money in one particular company's stock. In many cases this occurs because the investor works for the company and perhaps receives the company stock as a bonus or incentive or even as a match inside a 401(k).*

reasons. I've had people tell me all sorts of justifications for why they feel alright about having one large holding in one company.

There seems to be an underlying belief for people who choose to invest heavily in one company that this particular company has been around forever and isn't going anywhere. This is a huge mistake: Although I'm only 48 years old, off the top of my head I can name a few companies that used to be large and profitable but ran into major problems or disappeared altogether: Enron, WorldCom, Mirant, Fruit of the Loom, Arthur Andersen, Lehman Brothers, Wachovia, International Harvester, Penn Central Railroad, Johns-Manville, Polaroid, Xerox, Wang Laboratories, Control Data, among others.

Still, I keep hearing, "No ... I want to keep this stock" or "I know you're right, I do have too much with this one company, but I'm just not ready to sell it now" and of course one of my favorites, "I know I should diversify, but I don't want to have to pay the capital gains tax."

Lately following the deep market decline of 2008 to early 2009, I've heard that "diversification no longer works," right alongside with "the buy-and-hold strategy is dead!" I'd like to make an argument about those opinions.

At the top of the last bull market, which lasted from March 2003 until the late fall of 2007, many individual stocks had hit a record high. So did the Dow Jones Industrial Average and the S&P 500, two diversified market indexes. The two indexes are different: The DJIA has only 30 stocks, albeit in different industries, and the S&P 500 has, as its name implies, 500 stocks.

The DJIA topped out at around 14,160 in late 2007 and bottomed out in March 2009 around 6,550. That's a decline from peak to trough of roughly fifty-four percent.

The S&P 500 hit 1560 in 2007 and plummeted to 676 in March 2009, a drop of fifty-four percent; almost exactly the same percentage. Can we call these indexes diversified? Even my own deeply diversified, asset allocated index portfolios, representing more than 15,000 stocks, declined by fifty percent, from top to bottom. So it might lead one to believe that diversification no longer works.

But let's look at a few individual stocks, big names that we all know. And with each company, I will give the peak-to-trough numbers (in dollars) that generally were hit somewhere in early-to-mid 2007 and March 2009, so in all cases under a two-year time period.

- Citigroup—from 55 to 1.03. A decline of ninety-eight percent.

- Bank of America—from 51 to 3. A decline of ninety-four percent.

- AIG—from 51 to 1.5. A decline of ninety-eight percent (and that's with the huge government bailout).

- GE—from 42 to 6.6. A decline of eighty-four percent.

- Beazer Homes—from 35 to 0.29. A decline of ninety-nine percent (it had been at 70 a year before that).

- GM—from 42 to 1.2. A decline of ninety-seven percent.

- Delta—from 21 to 4. A decline of eighty-one percent.

It's arguable that I'm specifically picking companies that got killed in the meltdown, because they were financials or automotive or real estate sectors. But here are a few more:

- Marriott—from 47 to 13. A decline of seventy-two percent.

- Home Depot—from 41 to 18. A decline of fifty-six percent.

- AT&T—from 42 to 22. A decline of fifty-two percent.

- Southern Company—From 40 to 26. A decline of *only* thirty-four percent.

- Wal-Mart—from 63 to 46. A decline of *only* twenty-seven percent (hey, hey: I found a couple companies that beat the indexes).

And I'm sure if we search long and hard, we can find some companies that even made money during this economic train wreck. But here's my real message: Most people, including most brokers, do not pick the best companies most of the time. That's why we need a diversified portfolio, to reduce the risk of buying individual stocks.

Just investing in the U.S. large-cap market could have limited declines to around fifty-five percent from a potential of eight-five to ninety-nine percent. Try adding in some bonds and cash and a buy-and-hold portfolio of sixty percent stocks and forty percent bonds could have reduced declines to the twenty-five to thirty percent range from peak to trough.

The pundits who say, "Diversification no longer works," are wrong. It did work. It simply didn't reduce the entire downside risk, but no one ever promised it would.

The next story will tell of two people, one who followed the advice to diversify and one who didn't, and the results of each decision.

Too Many Shares of One Company's Stock—and Why that Can Be a Problem

We've all heard this tale of woe before: too much money in one company stock. Despite all the evidence that this lack of diversification can cause grave problems, there are many reasons investors find themselves in this situation:

- My father/mother worked for the company and I inherited the stock.

- My family always invested in _____ and it served them well.

- I work for the company, and the employer matching or bonus comes in shares of company stock.

- I know someone who made a lot of money in that stock/industry.

- I know it's too much, but I just don't want to pay the capital gains tax.

- Well this company is itself diversified since it's involved in so many different markets.

In the following story, we'll look at two individuals who had too much money in one company and needed to diversify.

I met Robert when he was about six months away from retirement. He had spent his working years in the not-for-profit business world and had been with one company for more than thirty years. He was 68 and married, with four grown children. He had never consulted with a financial planner before.

He had a decent net worth, including the following assets:

- $550,000 in retirement funds

- $190,000 in cash (Robert and his wife had been drawing Social Security while he continued to work and simply saving it!)

- $300,000 in WorldCom Stock (his wife had inherited it when it was worth around $30,000 from her father)

They also owned some land that they'd probably sell at some point, but the price and timing of the sale was unknown—certainly not by the time Robert retired.

For me, the WorldCom stock presented a problem, as it represented around 30 percent of their liquid net worth, which is way too much. I asked if they were sentimentally attached to the stock, and they said, no, but that they simply didn't know what they would do with it if they sold it. We discussed selling the bulk of the stock and they agreed. Although paying capital gains tax on the growth of $270,000 was not something they looked forward to, they recognized that it was safer in the long run to sell now. In addition, the current capital gains rate of fifteen percent was an all time low.

After discussing the sale of the stock with their CPA, they sold the WorldCom stock at about $53 a share. They reinvested the proceeds of the sale, less the $40,000 they needed to pay capital gains tax, and most of their cash (less what they needed for an emergency fund) into a diversified portfolio of sixty percent stock funds and forty percent bond funds, totaling $430,000.

The timing turned out to be perfect. WorldCom, one of the largest telecommunications firms at that time in the United

States, was hit big by mismanagement and had to announce that it was looking to sell out or fold. Needless to say, the stock price fell to under $5 a share virtually overnight.

This was at a time of substantial stock market declines across the board, so Robert's diversified portfolio did fall from $430,000 to $322,000. Yet if he had not sold the WorldCom when he did, the entire portfolio, including the cash, would have been worth around $190,000. Clearly diversification worked for Robert and his wife.

My next story involves a woman who had worked many years for General Electric. Most of her bonuses and incentives came in the form of stock. Although she had had numerous jobs after leaving GE, she always held on to the GE stock.

She died unexpectedly at age 50, and I met her widower, Marvin, in late 2007. He showed me a list of their assets prior to her death:

- $300,000 in her retirement funds

- $200,000 in his retirement funds, still held by his employer

- $300,000 in cash, around $200,000 of which was from the payout of life insurance on his wife

- $600,000 worth of GE stock (around 16,600 shares priced at about $36/share)

The great news was that Marvin was fine financially, thanks to his assets and his continued income from his job as construction superintendent. With his home paid off, he earned more than enough to make ends meet and was planning on working at least five to ten more years.

I immediately explained to him the danger of having more than forty percent of his money invested in one company. He admitted he knew this and was aware he needed to diversify. However, the dilemma when someone dies, especially so suddenly, is that it can be extremely difficult to make decisions when you are so emotionally overwhelmed. It was a year before he was ready to take action.

Since the stock was titled in his deceased wife's name, there was an enormous amount of paperwork to get the stock reregistered and deposited into an account. By this time it was almost the beginning of the fourth quarter of 2008, and the financial meltdown

I immediately explained to him the danger of having more than forty percent of his money invested in one company. He admitted he knew this and was aware he needed to diversify. ... It was a year before he was ready to take action.

had occurred. GE's stock value had fallen by sixty-four percent. That stock, valued at $600,000 when Marvin first came to see me, fell to only $220,000 in value (valuation as of the day I'm writing this section of the book).

Marvin should be fine, as he intends to keep working for a while. Also he's lucky that over his working years, he and his wife had still accumulated assets now worth around $1 million. But the bulk of that investment loss is due to the one overweighted position of GE stock he had in his portfolio. Yes, if he had sold the stock and reinvested, he still would have been down around fifteen to twenty percent. (We wouldn't have gone into an all-stock portfolio, so he wouldn't have experienced the entire 2008 stock market decline.)

Lessons Learned

1. Having a portfolio heavily overweighted in one stock can lead to financial devastation.

2. No one likes to pay capital gains taxes, but the alternative—watching a stock plummet—can be much worse.

3. Don't put off diversification. You never know when the company or sector you are overweighted in will get hit.

It's Just Money
So Why Does It Cause So Many Problems?

Sometimes we get attached to companies for the wrong reasons, and it hurts us later.

Too Many Shares of One Type of Stock—and Why that Can Be a Problem

Recently, a business associate came to me to discuss his father's financial situation. His father was in his late sixties, married, with three grown children. He had a home in a nearby mountain community and had retired after a lifetime of working in the banking industry.

Because of his deep knowledge of banking and his trust and belief in our banking system, this man had built his life savings by investing in bank stocks. He perceived banking institutions as strong, and their stocks likely to pay handsome dividends.

He felt diversified because he didn't own stock in only one bank. In fact, his portfolio, worth between $4 and $5 million dollars, held at least ten different financial institutions. More impressive, the portfolio paid around $200,000 in dividends annually. He and his wife were enjoying a wonderful retirement. They also drew Social Security and a small pension, but these truly were a pittance when compared with those dividends.

Of course, 2008 saw a slow decline of stock portfolios across the board. But when the situation became really bad in the fall of that year, starting with the fall of Lehman Brothers, the financial industry was hit the hardest. Many bank stocks fell by over ninety percent during this time. It was at this point my business associate shared with me his concern for his father. He told me that currently the portfolio was worth around $800,000 and his father and he were worried about the *possible* decline of dividend income. Possible decline? I told him *probable* was much more likely. In fact, by spring 2009, virtually all the father's dividend income had been deeply cut back or completely cut off—at least for the time being.

What options did his father have? In my book only one, but it's not one he would want to hear —adjusting his lifestyle to match the new income. As I write this section of the book, the portfolio has gained some value back, equating to around $1.5 million. With a diversified portfolio that size, he can reasonably create a sustainable income stream of around $60,000 a year. With Social Security and the small pension, he could bring that income up to around $90,000 a year. Many people in this country would love to have an income of $90,000 a year, especially during retirement when you are done with the expenses of raising children, and your mortgage is probably paid off.

But if human nature is my guide, I believe that after living the lifestyle afforded by $200,000 in dividend income, Mom and Dad will not be able to make the transition necessary to change their expenses.

The amount of stress and anxiety this situation has caused my friend's father is unfathomable to me; it's especially hard to have this kind of worry over money in your late sixties. ... I heard recently that his father was planning on trading stock to make money.

The amount of stress and anxiety this situation has caused my friend's father is unfathomable to me; it's especially hard to have this kind of worry over money in your late sixties. One would think it would be an easy decision to just find a reasonable house and a lifestyle you could afford. I heard recently that his father was planning on trading stock to make money.

All I could think about when I heard this, was how much more stress can this man take? Day Trading, the action of daily making buy and sell decisions on a stock or bond portfolio, is not for most people. I wouldn't recommend it to even the most savvy investor.

Unfortunately, it looks like this bad investing lesson is going to continue to the next generation. My friend also shared his own investing habits with me, so I am able to see the patterns of investing that he learned from his father. His own investment accounts are a variety of individual stocks, with banking stocks making up a disproportionate amount of the overall allocations. In addition, at the beginning of 2009, when the bank stocks were in the tank and the overall economy was hitting bottom, my friend closed a huge business deal and came into several hundred thousand dollars.

He bragged to me about the quick profit he had made in his bank stocks. I probed a little deeper, because I didn't understand, as I thought he had held these stocks for the long term and suffered substantial losses. It turns out that my friend took his business profits and invested them in these bank stocks that were *currently such a great deal.*

Again, I asked, "but isn't that profit from the business deal your cash flow for the next six months? Why would you invest that at all?" Of course, he admitted it was a risky move, but he felt the stocks had been beaten so low, he could make a quick profit. I sighed, and over the next couple of days watched as those stocks fell even further. My friend became nervous, and eventually sold at a substantial loss. Two to three months later most of those stocks hit bottom and came back, growing by fifty to one hundred percent or more. If he had held on, he could have made that short-term profit.

But day trading with short-term savings doesn't work. Emotionally we can't handle the volatility, because we really need that money. It's just gambling by another name, which is not what investing is all about.

Lessons Learned

1. Diversification is about a lot more than owning stock in more than one company, because when one sector falls, most of the companies within that sector are falling. It's about branching out into different sectors and different instruments, such as fixed income.

2. The only way to approach investing is rationally. Emotional attachments to particular stocks or sectors are a recipe for financial disaster.

3. Do not confuse investing with day trading. Timing the market over the short term is rarely a profitable exercise, especially when it's money you need.

It's Just Money
So Why Does It Cause So Many Problems?

Sometimes we let our heart or emotions rule our head.

Diversification can be thought of as spreading your investment dollars into various asset classes to add balance to your portfolio. Although it doesn't guarantee a profit, it may be able to reduce the volatility of your portfolio.

Investing in Real Estate is Not a Sure Thing

For years, it seemed impossible to go wrong in real estate. Some people simply owned their own homes and watched the equity grow through price appreciation, while others actually made a living buying and flipping houses. Unfortunately, there really is no such thing as a workable get rich quick scheme.

Nancy, age 50, and Richie, age 56, lived in California before moving to Alabama. They owned a nice home in California and had built up some decent equity. Nancy was a corporate executive earning $180,000 per year while Richie worked as a project manager earning $60,000.

In their neighborhood in California, townhouses such as the one they owned were selling for around $400,000 and the prices had risen so steadily that they had $125,000 in equity in their home. Around the corner was a townhouse almost identical to theirs, which had just come on the market for $359,000. There was nothing wrong with the home other than the horrible paint job that usually stopped prospective buyers at the foyer.

Nancy and Richie thought, "This will be easy; we can buy it, paint it, sell it and probably within thirty days turn this into a $20,000 profit even after the agent's commission!" They were short on cash, but knew they could borrow the down payment from a friend.

Simultaneously, Richie was offered a job in Alabama for a bit more pay with a great company, so they bought the distressed condo and, while Nancy got the painting done, Richie found them a new home in Alabama. Since their equity had risen so nicely, Richie settled on a house selling for $559,000—an upgrade from their California townhouse. They were able to put down twenty percent with the equity from the old home. They then took out an equity line of credit on the new house to pay back the friend.

As with so many things in life, timing is everything. They didn't realize they had bought at the top of the real estate market, and when they went to list their investment townhouse for sale, prices had modestly fallen. They figured, "How long can this downturn possibly last?" so they decided to rent it for a while.

Richie moved to start the new job while Nancy stayed behind and tried to get the townhouse rented. She did finally rent the townhouse, but the going market for rent was around $1,800 a month. The bad news was the monthly mortgage was $2,400 a month. A $600 a month deficit seemed like something they could handle for a year while the real estate market settled down. But real estate continued to decline, and finally plummeted. In the meantime, Nancy was unable to find a job in Alabama, so the small deficit of $600 a month now became a burden.

When they came to me for help, their current home in Alabama had a primary mortgage outstanding of $440,000 and a maxed out equity line of $100,000. The home's appraised value was now under $500,000. The investment townhouse in California had a primary mortgage of $324,000 and the appraised value was now under $300,000. They'd accumulated $35,000 in credit card debt over three years. The good news is they still had around $200,000 in retirement funds.

Unfortunately, I had little help to give. Refinancing was not feasible because they owed more on both properties than either was worth. The saddest part of this story was here was a couple who had never done any crazy investing in their life and just wanted to try what everyone else was having such luck at: flipping real estate.

If they had come to me earlier, I would have told them that an investment property is not viable if you have to borrow the down payment and can't afford to carry it if it doesn't sell. In addition, I would have explained they were overspending on their new home in Alabama, since they assumed that Nancy would find work. They should have bought a house they could afford on Richie's income alone or rented for a bit until Nancy found work. They probably weren't managing bills appropriately either; they were accumulating credit card debt.

Unfortunately, I had little help to give. ... The saddest part of this story was here was a couple who had never done any crazy investing in their life and just wanted to try what everyone else was having such luck at: flipping real estate.

My advice—although I didn't like having to give it—was to short sell the townhouse, spend a year paying down credit card debt, and then start to rebuild.

Booms never last. This was so reminiscent of 1999 when even I succumbed to the dot-com bull market and thought, "Why don't I buy some technology stocks like everyone else and make some quick cash!" I bought Cisco, Sun Microsystems, and Lucent, just to name a few, and lost my shirt on them all when the bottom fell out of the technology sector. The difference though was I borrowed *nothing* to do those purchases and the sum total of my investment was around $10,000, which I could certainly handle losing at the time.

For Nancy and Richie, this was a $100,000 mistake from which it will take them many years to recover.

Lessons Learned

1. No investment is a "sure thing." Be sure you won't find yourself financially devastated if things don't work out.

2. Buy a home you can afford, not a home you can afford *if* certain things work out.

3. Timing the market is almost always a losing proposition in any sector, including Real Estate.

It's Just Money
So Why Does It Cause So Many Problems?

We are poor judges of risk and make investment "bets" we can't really afford to lose.

The Magic of Compound Interest

Another great concept I wish I could get all my young clients to grasp is the magic of compound interest. It's exciting to learn how powerful it really is.

Consider that at a ten percent rate-of-return compounded annually a $10,000 investment will quadruple in fifteen years and be worth $40,000. But what if you kept the money invested for another fifteen years? ... The money would quadruple again to $160,000. It's the last fifteen years in the thirty-year block where the rocket ship of compounding returns really takes off. Stop and re-read this paragraph. Let this sink in for a minute before reading any further. (We are not in any way implying that a 10% return is reasonable, just that it makes the math easy.)

Here's another way to think about it: If you want to retire at age 55, your most important years of savings are from age 25 to 40, when most people are just starting to earn money and want to buy, buy, buy. If you are in that age bracket, resist the urge to spend, spend, spend and instead save, save, save. Think about those last fifteen years of saving and compounding in the example I gave in the paragraph above. It's kind of like creating a snowball that gets bigger and bigger the longer it's rolling, compacting and compounding, so the sooner you get started and the longer you compound the "snowball" the bigger your long-term retirement account might be.

If you start building your "snowball" later in life, at age 40 and above, you'll be trying to play catch up, and won't get the benefit of all that earlier time of compounding returns. In essence you will have to double or triple the amount you must save to reach the same goal.

My husband Ken and I decided years ago to commit to having savings and investments, exclusive of our house. To accomplish this we always have had to live beneath our means.

Nevertheless, even we have found it hard to stick to a long-term investment strategy. The first challenge came in 2000 through 2002 with the dotcom bubble bursting and bringing with it a decline of the entire U.S. stock market.

We watched our investments fall by over 30%. As much as we wanted to cut our losses and pull everything out of the market, we kept investing during the downturn. With the market growth of 2003 through 2006, we not only rebounded but also greatly exceeded our original high-water marks.

The next major test in our investing lives occurred during this most recent economic meltdown, with major declines starting in late 2007 and the market bottoming out and starting to rebound on March 9, 2009. We all watched the Dow go from well over 14,000 to a low of 6500.

In late 2008, our personal investments were down around 40%, now representing *substantial* dollar declines. Ken reminded me that if we had decreased our market exposure near the top of the stock market, we could have bought his log cabin dream home outright.

To be quite frank, in March 2009, I didn't have the stomach to actually count how low our personal dollars had dropped. I knew the losses would add up to more than I could bear to look at (on paper). Why put myself through the agony of looking at it? Logically and academically, I knew it was temporary, but even with twenty-three years professional experience, I am an emotional creature like any other human.

During this time, I decided to give each and every one of my clients the choice to update their financial plan, or take a year off of actually looking at the net worth statement if they didn't want to get depressed. We weren't sticking our heads in the sand. We knew what was going on. We still met and had our annual review as normal. We were just managing our emotions around our money, and in many cases, the decision to not look at the investments at the low point helped the majority stick to their long-term investment strategy.

Another important detail is that as a fee-based financial planner, my income is directly tied to my clients' account values so I was also looking at about a thirty-five percent to fifty percent loss of income, going forward indefinitely, until things turned around. I was irritated and frustrated by the ups and downs of the markets, but thankfully I was not worried about the decline in income because we hadn't overextended ourselves.

I'd like to point out something interesting that has occurred to me during this last market decline:

From a logical point of view, if you have a forty percent decline in a portfolio, then it goes as follows:

- $1,000 drops to $600 (a drop of $400, the price of a computer)

- $100,000 drops to $60,000 (a drop of $40,000, and that's the price of a very nice car)

- $1,000,000 drops to $600,000 (a drop of $400,000, and that's the price of a very nice house)

The percentage is the same, but for some reason, the bigger the dollar amount of the investment, the worse *the exact same percentage decline* seems to hurt. This is because money is emotional not just logical. Someone with $1000 invested might brush away a forty percent market loss saying, "Oh, well—it's just $400 and I've only just begun to feather my nest." Someone with $1 million in investments on the other hand might feel more of a sinking feeling when they look at their overall portfolio and see that a forty percent decline equals, gulp, $400,000.

The percentage is the same, but for some reason, the bigger the dollar amount of the investment, the worse **the exact same percentage decline** *seems to hurt. This is because money is emotional not just logical.*

Personally, since the 2008/09 market meltdown, I have found myself unwilling to take the same level of risk in my investments, probably because Ken and I have accumulated more serious dollar amounts and, as we push up to the big 5-0 birthdays, we are closer and closer to retirement age.

In thinking about all this, I go back to my childhood. How am I affected by my upbringing? I learned the value of a dollar. I learned that buying the exact same thing at a lower price was both logical and also exhilarating. I learned to save and invest in the markets and not to be scared of the inherent volatility. During any market decline, I can still call my father and he will reassure me that this too shall pass because, at eighty-one years old, he's seen this many times before (and I'm so grateful he is still with me today to offer his sage advice).

During 2009, the year of the Ponzi scheme du jour, my father lost $50,000 in one such investment. I asked him how he felt about this and he said, "You know Karen, you win some and you lose some." His wisdom will live on through me and, hopefully, his grandchildren long after he is gone.

I still catch myself struggling with the concept of "It's Just Money". So I try to remember on a daily basis, in spite of what the market is doing and how much money we have, that regardless, life is good!

Chapter 15
Final Words to the Wise

Money problems abound today, but we should all remember that they have also plagued other generations. Of course the problems are different generation to generation based on economic conditions. Nevertheless, problems will continue to exist in our lives. For each of us individually, money problems are both a product of the way we were raised and the reaction to the things that have happened in our adult lives. Good or bad, we all have a relationship with money that deserves to be examined.

If you read this book, I'm guessing you are either have money problems in your life and are looking for some answers, or perhaps you know someone who is struggling with money and you are trying to help. You've read the stories in this book, and you've most likely identified with a few of them. So what do you do now?

Six Steps to Transform your Money Life

Write a money autobiography. What are your earliest childhood recollections about money and how do those mental tapes still play out in your life today? What has happened along the way in your working years that has impacted how you feel about money today? This exercise can greatly enhance your awareness of your unique relationship to money.

Admit that a problem exists. The first step in fixing any problem is awareness that a problem exists. So you've taken the first step by reading this book and relating to the stories. You have or are becoming aware of why you (or your friends, colleagues and loved ones) have money problems in the first place. Hopefully you might even feel some relief. You now know that it's not that you are simply bad with money, or lacking intelligence, but that you really weren't taught good money skills growing up, and/or over the years developed bad habits due to certain circumstances.

Tell it all to someone you trust. When people attempt to overcome addiction or change bad habits, they must first admit to themselves that they have a problem, and then become willing to share that admission with a trusted counselor. This is the principle of honesty, and sometimes the hardest person to be honest with is yourself. So your next step is to choose a trusted friend, parent, clergy member or counselor and come clean on what you now know about yourself in relationship to money. Be prepared to really open up and bare all. It helps to be gut wrenchingly honest.

Make a plan and get into action. Now comes the really hard work: Making a game plan and taking some action. Remember, this will not be easy, and it will not happen overnight. You will have setbacks. Remember that a healthy relationship to money is analogous to diet and exercise. The crash diet never works, but the lifestyle changes that are forever do work. When you cheat on a diet, it's not wise to throw in the towel and give up. Try to get back on your plan the next day. Changing money habits will be a similar journey. Two steps forward, one step back. DON'T GIVE UP!

Believe in yourself. Have faith in yourself that you can change. You can adopt better money behaviors. People choose to make changes in their behavior all the time! People who have been sedentary their whole lives start exercising. Alcoholics and other addicts give up their addictions. Smokers quit smoking. You can do it too. We *all* have the capacity to change, if we really want to, especially if the things we are trying to change about ourselves are impacting the quality of our lives, our happiness and well being.

Visualize prosperity. Consider the trouble that your money issues have brought into your life, and envision a future that looks different. Imagine how it would feel to be free of debt, or have a nest egg to fall back on. Wouldn't it be incredible to no longer worry about the loss of a job, an emergency home or car repair?

Think of how your relationships with people could grow if you no longer fought over money, or had money issues come between friendships and family. Think of the happiness of being able to buy something you really want and deserve and not have to worry about how to pay for it.

Final words to the wise? There is light at the end of the tunnel. You can lift the stress that your money problems have caused you. You deserve to be free of money baggage forever. Take the next step now!

My Personal Reflections

About the Author

Karen J. Lee of Karen Lee and Associates, LLC in Atlanta, Georgia, has worked in the financial services industry since 1987. During this time she has worked with hundreds of families, individuals, and small businesses in helping them to work towards their financial dreams. She has the comprehensive education and experience to handle all aspects of a person's financial situation.

Karen J. Lee, CFP®, CLU, ChFC, MSFS, AEP
Financial Planner

As evidence of this, Karen holds various licenses and registrations in the areas of insurance, securities, and investment planning.

Karen Lee and Associates is a proud member of Integrated Financial Group, a consortium of independent financial advisors. This group of financial planners share their knowledge, tools, and experiences to benefit the clients of the entire consortium.

- She is a CERTIFIED FINANCIAL PLANNER™ professional and has earned her Chartered Life Underwriter and Chartered Financial Consultant designations.

- She holds a Master of Architecture from Tulane University and a Master of Science in Financial Services from the American College.

- She also holds the Accredited Estate Planner designation.

- She is a regular guest on CNN.

- She has been quoted in articles for *Kiplinger's, Forbes, MSN Money Central, CNBC.com, AICPA Wealth Management Insider, Financial Planning* magazine, *Parenting* magazine, and more.

In addition to working with clients in her financial planning practice, Karen enjoys speaking and teaching financial strategies to different groups. She is a member of the Financial Planning Association and the National Estate Planning Council. Karen and her husband, Ken, currently live in Georgia, with their son, Daniel, and daughter, Julia, and many pets. Karen and her family enjoy sailing, boating, reading, and all outdoor activities.